Sylvia

W9-BMD-508

BUSINESS PARTNERING FOR CONTINUOUS IMPROVEMENT

BUSINESS PARTNERING FOR CONTINUOUS IMPROVEMENT

How to Forge Enduring Alliances Among Employees, Suppliers & Customers

CHARLES C. POIRIER

&

WILLIAM F. HOUSER

Berrett-Koehler Publishers
San Francisco

Amsterdam • Johannesburg • London
San Diego • Sydney • Toronto

Copyright © **1993 by Charles C. Poirier**
All rights reserved. No part of this publication may be reproduced, distributed, or transmitted in any form or by any means, including photocopying, recording, or other electronic or mechanical methods, without the prior written permission of the publisher, except in the case of brief quotations embodied in critical reviews and certain other noncommercial uses permitted by copyright law. For permission requests, write to the publisher, addressed "Attention: Permissions Coordinator," at the Berrett-Koehler address below.

Berrett-Koehler Publishers, Inc.   **Pfeiffer & Company**
155 Montgomery St.   8517 Production Avenue
San Francisco, CA 94104–4109   San Diego, CA 92121

Ordering Information
Orders by individuals and organizations. This book is available through bookstores or can be ordered direct from either publisher at the addresses above.

Quantity sales. Berrett-Koehler publications are available at special quantity discounts when purchased in bulk by corporations, associations, and others. For details, write to the "Special Sales Department" at the Berrett-Koehler address above or call (415) 288–0260.

Orders by U.S. trade bookstores and wholesalers. Please contact Prima Worldwide, P.O. Box 1260, Rocklin, CA 95677–1260; tel. (916) 786–0426; fax (916) 786–0488.

Orders for college textbook/course adoption use. Please contact Berrett-Koehler Publishers, 155 Montgomery St., San Francisco, CA 94104–4109; tel. (415) 288–0260; fax (415) 362–2512.

Printed in the United States of America

Printed on acid-free and recycled paper that meets the strictest state and U.S. guidelines for recycled paper (50 percent recycled waste, including 10 percent postconsumer waste).

Credits are on page 247.

Library of Congress Cataloging-in-Publication Data

Poirier, Charles C., 1936–
    Business partnering for continuous improvement : how to forge enduring alliances among employees, suppliers & customers / Charles C. Poirier & William F. Houser. – 1st ed.
    p. cm.
    Includes bibliographical references and index.
    ISBN 1-881052-10-9 (hardcover : alk. paper) : $29.95
    1. Industrial management. 2. Organizational change.
3. Communication in management. 4. Public relations. I. Houser, William F., 1940–   . II. Title.
HD31.P56   1993
658.4–dc20
    92–23473
    CIP

First Edition
Second Printing August 1993

Book Production: Pleasant Run Publishing Services
Composition: Classic Typography

To Monte R. Haymon,
who gave us the workshop
in which to prove the validity
of our ideas

Contents

Preface

Today, virtually every American firm of any size has an improvement process under way. The efforts vary in concept, direction, intensity, and reward, but they are all focused on achieving better performance. Organizations throughout the nation are chasing lower costs, higher quality, better service, more throughput, higher levels of customer satisfaction, lower inventories, shorter cycle times, or some combination of these elements of business. The names for the chosen process may vary, but the astute firms in America are seeking significant improvement to the ways in which they conduct business. To have no improvement effort under way is tantamount to losing ground since so many companies are moving forward.

For the past decade, we have been immersed in this effort, concentrating on improvement to all facets of business. Our interests and professional assignments have included manufacturing and service groups, sales forces, administrative staffs, engineers, and researchers. The size of the groups have ranged from less than a million dollars of annual sales to over a billion dollars per year. Our immersion has covered the full business spectrum. Through a concerted sharing of information, we are now in possession of a large portfolio describing what is being attempted in American business as leaders search for better performance. The results from these efforts are so mixed that almost any argument can be presented regarding how to be successful. Since one of our major concerns was how to achieve success across all parts of the organization, we studied those documented attempts and their supporting arguments. We patiently took the time to see if they contained the missing ingredients we sought. We now conclude that the listener to such arguments must be alert to separating fact from fiction—and hard results from good intentions. In *Business Partnering for Continuous Improvement,* we endeavor to draw out those distinctions.

Our Portfolio

Our portfolio of articles, documents, books, and recorded conversations on improvement efforts includes hundreds of references. We studied over fifty organizations considered leading-edge companies, including Toyota, Nissan, Sanyo, Corning, TRW, Rohm and Haas, Baxter, Westinghouse, Hewlett-Packard, Florida Power and Light, Northern Telecom, McDonnell Douglas, Ford, Motorola, Campbell Soup Company, IBM, Moore, Procter & Gamble, Vitro of Mexico, and many others. We have visited over fifty sites where successful improvement efforts were reported. We have communicated firsthand with individuals and organizations involved in major change processes. Our travels have taken us to see such Japanese organizations as Sanyo, Matsushita, Toyota, Nissan, and Honda. We studied all the Baldrige Award winners and companies that applied the latest improvement techniques. The information we gained was added to the pertinent literature to form the portfolio we reference.

Through analysis and field checking, we found information that contained genuine, sustained results that we gladly share, with permission from the sources. We found a larger number of stories that detail what people intended to accomplish rather than what was actually achieved. In brief, we offer to the reader the best advice we could glean from existing results, our application experiences, and the testing of nearly every idea that made sense.

Why We Wrote This Book

During our involvement in leading, directing, and coordinating improvement efforts, we discovered a wealth of valuable information from which we borrowed to augment our endeavors. And we developed our portfolio, which we have just described. However, we had difficulty finding ways to resolve three major concerns:

- How to overcome the resistance that impeded the implementation of logical improvement concepts, across the full spectrum of an organization
- How to inspire individuals within an organization to continuously pursue and achieve stretch objectives to attain a true competitive advantage
- How to sustain improvements over the long term

Our learning experiences and the conviction that many others responsible for improving business operations have similar concerns caused us to write this book. We do not find in the business literature the description of a continuous improvement process, generic enough that it will be successful for all situations. We fail to find how to overcome the full range of obstacles we know serve to inhibit implementation and the achievement of stretch goals. Nor do we find the secrets of sustaining improvement gains. It is our intention to present a guidebook that will fill these voids.

Intended Audience

This book was written for people in business who have been frustrated in their search for continuous improvement, world-class status in their market, some form of competitive advantage, or the means to sustain whatever improvements have been achieved. We not only show how to use sensible alliances for achieving long-term success but also provide extensive, useful examples of what works and—more important for the frustrated reader—what does *not* work, and why.

This book will appeal to those seeking sound improvement advice and illustrates applications in manufacturing and service industries, in all business disciplines, and for all positions—from supervisors through managers to executives and leaders of the business community. Lastly, our efforts will bring fresh insights to all who are attempting to strengthen their supplier-to-consumer chain, what we term the *partnering network*.

Overview of the Contents

We present two themes in this book—continuous improvement and business partnering. Our first argument is that continuous improvement—focusing on quality, productivity, and profit improvement—must be created and sustained throughout an organization. Our second argument is that the establishment of mutual alliances—business partnering, in our terminology—has to occur first within the organization and then be extended to suppliers and customers to sustain the improvement gains and secure a competitive advantage.

In Chapter One, we examine the need for improvement efforts and discuss why such efforts often fail to achieve their goals. We introduce continuous improvement and business partnering as successful business strategies for the 1990s. Chapter Two presents the continuous improvement model, which is an integrated system that requires a concurrent focus on quality, productivity, and profit improvement. In Chapter Three, we describe business partnering—the building of alliances for mutual benefit throughout an organization's business network. We argue that business partnering is the key for successful, enduring improvement efforts.

Chapter Four begins the transition from theory to practice. Here we describe the critical role that management must play in the execution of an improvement effort. We believe that the logical first place to begin an improvement effort is within the organization, and Chapter Five shows how to get started. We present tools and techniques to translate objectives and plans into an operating strategy. Chapter Six examines the obstacles and resistance to successful application of a continuous improvement effort and how they must be overcome.

Chapter Seven shows how to develop the partnering concept within the organization and proposes employee involvement as the vehicle for this journey. The necessity of forming mutually beneficial alliances with suppliers is covered in Chapter Eight. Business partnering is the methodology by which outside help is secured to enhance and sustain the accomplishments of the improvement effort. In Chapter Nine, we close the loop by illustrating how to include customers in the full partnering network. Chapter Ten summarizes how the process becomes a reality.

Since we believe valuable learning occurs through studying both successes and failures, we use examples and illustrations throughout this book that show where improvement worked and where it did not. As we develop our arguments, we fit appropriate examples to the points under discussion. We also include anecdotes that we assure the reader are very close to real-life situations. We have created a near-to-life heroine, Alice Harper, who helps demonstrate the application of our principle. Each chapter includes an appropriate action study to illustrate how existing organizations have attempted to implement the concepts being discussed.

Acknowledgments

We especially want to thank Steven Piersanti of Berrett-Koehler Publishers for his continual encouragement and help in bringing our work to fruition. We also thank Mary Garrett, who edited the manuscript and managed its production. Her help was invaluable to two novice writers. Thanks also to Barbara Santeler, who worked tirelessly to prepare and retype the many drafts of the manuscript. Many others contributed valuable ideas to the content of the book, and we have attempted to recognize their help in the text.

Evanston, Illinois   Charles C. Poirier
Houston, Texas   William F. Houser
August 1992

The Authors

Charles C. Poirier is Senior Vice-President—Quality and Productivity for Packaging Corporation of America (PCA). He is responsible for directing PCA's continuous improvement process and the company's drive for total customer satisfaction through quality performance. He is also a member of the company's management committee.

Poirier joined PCA in 1984 to take charge of quality and productivity improvement. Under his leadership, PCA initiated its successful and precedent-setting Excellence in Manufacturing Program and its internal and external partnering process. During his tenure, he has served as Senior Vice-President—Manufacturing and as Group Vice-President of PCA's aluminum and plastics business unit.

With thirty-four years experience in various technical and management positions, Poirier is well known as a speaker and writer on industry topics. Prior to joining PCA, he was Chief Engineer, Director of Manufacturing, Area General Manager, and Director of Marketing and Sales for the Container Division of St. Regis Paper Company.

Poirier received his B.S. degree (1958) in industrial management from Carnegie Mellon University and his M.B.A. degree (1966) from the University of Pittsburgh.

William F. Houser is Director of Productivity and Quality for Tenneco, Inc. In this capacity, he is responsible for helping the Tenneco companies (J.I. Case, Case IH, Packaging Corporation of America, Walker Muffler, Monroe Shock Absorber,

Albright and Wilson, and Newport News Shipbuilding) in their productivity and total quality management initiatives.

Prior to joining Tenneco in 1985, Houser held quality, product service, operations, and general management positions in diverse industries, including consumer and capital goods, automotive, electronics, ordnance, and aerospace.

Houser has published papers in several national publications and is a frequent speaker, having spoken at the national conventions of the American Society for Quality Control (ASQC) and the Institute of Industrial Engineers.

Houser received his B.S. degree (1962) in electrical engineering from Tri State College in Indiana. He is a registered professional engineer in quality and an ASQC-certified quality engineer.

Chapter One

◆

WHY CONTINUOUS IMPROVEMENT AND BUSINESS PARTNERING?

American business is not keeping pace with the rest of the world. While U.S. productivity is increasing, studies conducted by General Systems Company show that it is growing at "half the average rate of ten years ago. Foreign competitors have been making gains three or four times as large in those same years" (Feigenbaum, 1991, p. 69). The World Competitiveness Report is published each year by the International Institute for Management Development and the World Economic Forum, both located in Geneva, Switzerland. The 1991 report, which covers thirty-seven industrialized countries, shows the United States is fifth on their "overall competitiveness scoreboard," ranking behind Japan, Germany, Switzerland, and Denmark. The U.S. ranking in the 1990 report was second place. The *International Productivity Journal* ("Statistical Comparisons," 1991, p. 78) lists the following results for real labor productivity growth rate in Gross Domestic Product (GDP) per employee (1981–88):

Country	Growth Rate (in percentage)
Japan	2.9
United Kingdom	2.6
France	2.0
Canada	1.8
Belgium	1.7
U.S.	1.3

1

Current business journals also chronicle the consistent progress being made by foreign competitors. In spite of impressive stories about domestic organizations that have successfully implemented major improvements and built the gains into their actions and business plans, global competition continues to force the need for more domestic improvement.

America is far from being out of the race, but it no longer commands a substantial lead.

What Happened to American Business?

Annual plans are a regular part of business discipline. We personally have participated in preparing many of these documents. In the decades of the 1960s and 1970s, it was usual in our world to submit these annual exercises with 3-5 percent projected improvements in all vital areas of the time — annual sales, material costs, delivery costs, labor costs per unit, number of new customers, and so forth. For our superiors, a fairly conservative improvement was acceptable, and inflation could be counted on to give the impression of progress. During a particularly tough time, the goals might be temporarily raised, but we eventually went back to the 3-5 range.

As U.S. leaders were content with strategic plans that proposed single-digit improvements, fostered modest gains in performance, and led to bonuses achieved more through favorable market conditions than breakthrough efforts, the rest of the world caught up, and some players in the new global competition breezed past. Deceived by the false concept that lower labor costs were fueling the impressive foreign gains, U.S. managers continued to submit plans with targets that were assured of accomplishment. Offshore, the plans contained double-digit goals and innovations intended to garner American customers. When the resultant lower costs, new products, and features were combined with short cycle times unheard of in this country, the flow of sales to foreign firms began in earnest.

While the masters of the automobile industry in Detroit pondered how to automate out the costly human factor, Taiichi Ohno (1986) at Toyota worked on how to overcome the U.S. advantage. By his calculation, General Motors and Ford had an eight times (8X) advantage in terms of productivity. In 1952, it took ten Toyota employees one month to produce one truck. He estimated that American producers could make eight trucks with the same human resources.

By applying his breakthrough concepts of *kanban* (parts delivered when needed in quantities needed), *poka-yoke* (fool-proofing system changes so that improvements are not lost), *andon* (a red light that comes on to signal a problem), and others, Ohno was able to substantially improve performance. In 1985, Toyota produced 250,000 trucks in one month with 45,000 employees. Since the starting point was .1 truck/employee/month and the new level was 5.5 trucks/employee/month, the magnitude of improvement was 55X. Any competitor, during this time frame, that was content with annual improvements of 3–5 percent would have fallen significantly behind, regardless of starting advantage.

During a similar period, Shigeo Shingo (1985) was reducing machine setup times from days to minutes. His book *A Revolution in Manufacturing: The SMED System* is a compendium of examples of how sensible use of employee time and effort, without major investments in new capital, can make improvements of 10X, 50X, even 100X possible. As he and his associates were pursuing these types of breakthroughs across Japanese businesses, managers in the U.S. were still accepting minor annual improvements as acceptable progress. They did not realize it, but they were treading water, using up their businesses' internal energy without providing for new energy.

The realization finally dawned that many U.S. firms were in trouble, and industry leaders began chasing competition—foreign and domestic—with a plethora of new concepts. Quality, productivity, benchmarking, just-in-time deliveries, *kaizen*, statistical process control, work cells, and a litany of alphabetical shorthand (SMED, OPT, CIMS, TQM, MRP, CAD-CAM) were used in the hunt. Peters and Waterman (1982) fueled the quest as they sent an army of readers in search of excellence. Eager managers went looking for a cookbook answer that would improve their operations, retain their customers, and secure their futures.

What these searchers found was that there is no simple solution. What works for one organization does not always guarantee success for another. The pursuit of quality, which has proven to be a great motivator, is a prime example. Organizations throughout the world have been inspired to make significant improvements to quality as people try their best to do the right things right. Unfortunately, based on our observations and conversations with hundreds of professional practitioners, these efforts seem to have a lifetime of about eighteen months. After that time, the activities wane and quality slips back to previous levels. Our experience is supported by a 1985 study by A. T. Kearney, a Chicago-based consulting firm, that showed that 83 percent of quality circles (an early improvement technique) were dropped within eighteen months of implementation.

An Example: Quality Improvement Efforts

We have talked with scores of managers and executives who have responsibility for running a company or division or for overseeing their firm's improvement process. Most of these individuals admit they have tried for a quick fix by attempting to apply a lockstep quality improvement process that appeared logical and had worked elsewhere. Without considering if the environmental circumstances were similar or if the organization members understood the necessary change in focus, they charged forward with enthusiasm and waited for quality to dramatically improve and profits to leap forward. Unfortunately, most of these managers and executives were disappointed with the results.

Middle managers gave their leaders assurances of their

dedication. They focused their attention, momentarily, on the prescribed orientation—quality improvement—and pledged their energies to implement the process. Like most of these improvement efforts, some early successes appeared as the novelty of the quality orientation created an atmosphere of earnest enthusiasm. The dedication proved to be cosmetic, however, so the desired results were not attained. In one case, for example, when it was discovered that, for reasons important to the parent company, quality would not extend to the primary source of raw material supplied by that parent, line supervisors began to lose their pledged interest. They dropped their intensity and went back to business as usual.

We have found that leaders often could not demonstrate or sustain a focused commitment to a singular improvement strategy—for example, quality—because they continued to give priority to matters of a short-term cost nature. The leaders created the initial emphasis on quality but never gave up their normal concern for other, more traditional areas of focus, such as growth and financial performance. These leaders endorsed a seemingly sure-bet orientation, without being prepared for any lukewarm implementation or the inevitable backlash. When faced with weak support, their confidence in the logic of the process wavered, and they shifted their focus to cost reduction or another area of concern they thought more readily controllable. When confronted with actual backlash, that is, some form of refusal to implement (for example, scrapping a poor-quality lot), the leader often acceded, sending a strong negative signal throughout the organization.

Subordinate managers can be equally ambivalent, as they have been trained to put profit and productivity improvement ahead of all other business considerations. Focusing on quality, even when it means accepting temporary cost increases or lowering output, conflicts with traditional values. Without consistent reinforcement from the top, managers will abandon their early, enthused endorsement and retreat to more comfortable areas of expertise and control.

Most important is that a focus on a singular improvement

strategy—even one as strong as quality—will not receive full acceptance or honest endorsement by those within the organization who must implement the changes. They withhold full support because such a limited orientation does not pay appropriate attention to all of the factors necessary to run a successful business. People need something more encompassing that contains insights into how to improve all the factors of a business, not just the quality of products and services. They need a focus that includes how to simultaneously reduce costs and raise productivity as they improve quality, thereby increasing profitability.

The end result of single-focus improvement efforts has become all too familiar. Leaders wander in their orientation and managers prefer a concentration on normal business activities. Without recognizing their role in the nonimplementation, perplexed leaders and subordinate managers review the mixed results and lack of sustained improvement and wonder—what went wrong?

The Dilemma of Nonimplementation

So what does go wrong? The need for improvement is so great and so well documented, and so many improvement efforts have been tried. Why haven't there been better results? Throughout this book we will detail the reasons for nonimplementation of these well-intentioned efforts. For the purpose of this introduction, we focus on the two most critical reasons: disoriented leadership and tubular thinking.

Disoriented Leadership

Most improvement efforts, based on quality or other factors, begin with an enthused introduction by the leaders of the organization, particularly the chief executive officer (CEO). These leaders endorse the guiding principles, stress the needs behind the efforts, and make an early commitment to strongly participate in guiding the process to success. The track records clearly show that most of these same leaders withdraw their support in favor of an orientation toward short-term necessities. Mergers, acquisitions, current emergencies, and unexpected market disruptions invariably are accorded higher priority. The hunt for improvement becomes secondary to the short-term orientation.

Leaders like Bob Galvin and David Kearns, who doggedly kept the improvement efforts alive at Motorola and Xerox, are the exception, not the rule. For each true success story we collected in our research on improvement efforts, there are a multitude of others where leaders lost their intensity. Favoring what they considered more important matters, these leaders transferred their attention to short-term, cost improvement. Organizations that chased the quality solution in the early to mid 1980s were often left with disenchanted workers who wondered what happened to all the enthusiasm and motivation.

The reality of the past decade's efforts is that American managers prefer a quick fix, often characterized by the inevitable downsizing in personnel. They talk at length of the merits of a long-term orientation, of the importance of quality, a customer focus, and innovation as critical to success, of their willingness to adopt successful ideas, and the fact that people are their most important assets. Such talk has a hollow sound to the growing thousands of displaced people who decry the lack of any semblance of consistency in their former organizations, where the "survive-the-month" attitude was worshipped in deference to long-term success. With the continuance of consolidation actions in nearly every industry—along with the usual clever financing that greatly increases the need for new cash flow to cover interest payments—we can only predict this dilemma will get worse. The solution to this problem requires that leaders develop a greater understanding of the criticality of their continued, oriented, and supportive posture as a factor in successful implementation of a *continuous* improvement process, which has now become a business imperative.

Tubular Thinking

Part of the blame for nonattainment of important objectives rests with disoriented leadership. The second factor for non-success is a characteristic of those directly below the senior offices. The typical U.S. manager suffers from tubular thinking, thinking that is characterized by an abundance of concern for a particular unit of an organization, rather than for the total organization. The manager of a tubular unit also has greater concern for his or her self-image and for satisfying a few leadership figures (who could affect career advancement) than in utilizing the help that could come from a sharing of resources across units. The tubular manager generally foregoes asking for outside help because of the absence of individual recognition for the effort or results.

This mentality is probably born of personal ambitions encouraged in our highly competitive culture and from our love for organizational charts, with the clearly defined turf that results from such block-by-block assignments of responsibility. It is a flawed perspective because the usual result is the creation of silo-like departments and operations that have little meaningful intercourse with other units within the same organization. The firm suffers under these conditions, and the chances for optimization are reduced because the potential synergies that could derive are never achieved.

Tubular thinking is not limited to internal organizational conditions; it is equally an external phenomenon. At "Quest for Excellence," the symposium sponsored in February 1991 by the American Society for Quality Control and the National Institute of Standards and Technology to feature the 1990 winners of the Malcolm Baldrige National Quality Award, this tubular characteristic was apparent. Over 1,500 attendees went to Washington, D.C., to learn how four business organizations had managed to win the coveted prize. As the winners shared their improvement ideas, concepts, and techniques with a generally enthralled audience, not one automobile manufacturer was there to take notes on Cadillac. These competitors remained inside their comfortable silos, content with the mistaken belief that any idea for improvement spawned outside of their silo could hardly be worth hearing. The not-invented-here-so-it-cannot-be-any-good syndrome prevented many auto producers from learning how to make what Cadillac showed were truly stretch improvements.

Horizontal thinking can break down the invisible walls that too often exist between what should be cooperating units. These walls serve to limit attention to factors that could enhance competitive successes. Only in times of crisis or under direct orders from a powerful CEO do we see U.S. managers forsake their usual myopic view of the value of cross-functional or cross-location cooperation. Reaching out for needed assistance occurs far more often as a last resort than as a preventive or improvement measure.

Our experience in working with numerous organizations, large and small, manufacturing and service oriented, has schooled us to expect middle-level managers to extol the virtues of team efforts but to secretly favor the promotion of individual performance, first, and unit performance, second. Consider the plant manager who has responsibility for a manufacturing facility that is duplicated at several geographical locations. If this individual suffers from the tubular malaise, he or she will consider seeking cooperation with other plant managers a sign of weakness and will forego the potential gain from focusing outside wisdom on a specific area of opportunity. Outside resources are also avoided because the silo manager fears the resulting analysis could launch a witch hunt to find those responsible for any lack of performance that may be discovered. This attitude is far too pervasive. Certain operations need help, which is resisted when offered—not because of any changes that might be required but out of fear of retribution for not finding the answers before the outside source reveals them.

How to Promote Progress

The picture is not completely bleak. Significant progress is occurring in some segments of U.S. business, providing a beacon to would-be followers. While the Japanese gather most of the attention, there are American firms making similar impressive gains. Joseph Juran (1991), the noted quality specialist, has introduced a dimension that separates exceptional improvement from ordinary improvement. Reviewing the recent winners of the Malcolm Baldrige National Quality Award—such firms as Milliken, Xerox, Motorola, IBM-Rochester, Cadillac, and Westinghouse Nuclear Fuel Division—he summarized how these organizations achieved impressive results:

> One obvious difference was that the companies established "stretch goals," such as:
> - Ten-fold quality improvement in four years
> - Four-fold improvements in reliability
> - Twelve-month reductions in the product development cycle
>
> Such quality goals cannot be met using the pedestrian pace of the ordinary learning curve. Something extraordinary is needed to meet stretch goals [1991, p. 82].

In remarking on what he considered "stunning results," Juran cited these typical performance improvements by the winners:

- Customer service response times reduced from days to hours
- Defect levels reduced up to 50 percent
- Productivity doubled
- Costs reduced by 50 percent

These measures certainly do not represent progress at a "pedestrian pace."

Business has become a global matter, and the competitors who are winning are doing so because they have made improvement their defining characteristic. We have watched with ever-increasing curiosity as foreign competitors, particularly the Japanese, have parlayed a consistent attention to stretch achievements, supported by team efforts, into greater sales and profit. For us, the challenge became how to surpass that kind of success in spite of our national reverence for individual performance. The answer has crystallized as a system of continuous pursuit of stretch objectives (continuous improvement), supported by a network of logical alliances (business partnering). The two themes we present in this book—continuous improvement and business partnering—illustrate how American business can catch those winning competitors and ultimately gain the lead in the race.

Continuous Improvement

Our basic argument is that continuous improvement—directed toward stretch objectives—must be created and sustained throughout the organization. Disoriented leadership and tubular thinking have to be overcome. It is ironic that after ten full years of trying to make improvement a way of life in American business, foreign competitors have gained an edge. As U.S. leaders continued to pursue their business-for-the-moment strategies, the Japanese steadfastly concentrated their orientation on using technology, quality, innovation, and people as the cornerstones for domination of world markets.

Continuous improvement must be integrated into all business systems within the organization, with double-digit objectives on an annual basis. In the ensuing chapters, we expand our argument as we establish that competitive advantage is achieved as business firms focus on a three-part, continuous effort that seeks stretch objectives in the areas of quality, productivity, and profit improvement. If a business organization is going to do more than keep pace, those within the organization have to improve performance in these three essential categories at a speed that exceeds the best competitors. This argument translates into conducting a pursuit of improvement as part of the nature of doing business. Anything less may sustain the firm for a while, but it is akin to treading water.

Business Partnering

Our second theme requires the building of alliances for mutual benefit throughout an organization's business network to sustain improvements and to create a competitive advantage. Why is partnering so important? Since we believe that business partnering is the real secret for gaining both success and endurance with improvement efforts, we will consider in this book what advantages partnering can bring to the process.

Understanding the importance of partnering and the advantages it offers to a continuous improvement effort came to us as much by chance as through any other circumstance. An example of what we encountered during a typical improvement effort will help explain. In the early 1980s, we were commissioned to work with a newly acquired subsidiary. This organization was a proud, profitable firm that had a recognized brand name and a loyal customer base. Improving profits on an annual basis was already part of its existing culture. Our assignment was to introduce a quality and productivity ethic that would enhance current levels of performance and generate additional profits to cover the cost of acquisition.

In this environment, we encountered enthusiasm and willing participation by the employees and managers. Applying the usual improvement tools and techniques, we were able to generate a significant reduction in setup times and to debottleneck the manufacturing process. The quality process that was introduced quickly raised the reliability level of incoming materials and dramatically reduced the need for inspectors, who previously removed the off-specification product that reached finished goods. Costs per unit dropped as increased volume was generated with a lower number of labor hours and fewer mistakes. Within a period of eighteen months, the processes that were implemented had been assimilated and the measurements clearly indicated the effort had been a success.

Unfortunately, the results were not fully sustained. As we had witnessed in other efforts, some gains leveled off while in a few areas there was backsliding to previous levels. As the senior-level drive for improvement relaxed and managers focused more on routine matters, all of the key measurements showed slowing trends toward higher performance. The situation was not unusual in our experiences, but it left us with the feeling that something important was missing from our repair kit. We reviewed our circumstances and saw the usual positive ingredients. But we did not see the binding ingredient that would hold the progress together and take it to the next higher level without forceful driving.

There was leadership present, along with cooperation, synergistic problem solving, focused attention, and the other ingredients necessary to make project-by-project improvements, but only for a moment. What eluded us was how to establish permanency: in the teams, the team effort, and the support of suppliers. We also sought an ingredient that would provide the kind of commitment to the customer that would secure long-term positions in an increasingly competitive environment. We could not identify this elusive commodity at first, but we were certain something existed that would resolve the disorientation that occurred as soon as the intensity eased and the group returned to silo thinking.

Shortly after this experience, we began at a few test sites to try forming some alliances with involved constituencies. We experimented with novel pacts between labor and management that included direct sharing in the improvement benefits. We solicited help from suppliers on quality and productivity efforts in exchange for larger, long-term positions. We developed workshops to increase synergistic efforts between sales and manufacturing departments. We conducted training sessions for leaders—oriented to a three-part quality, productivity, and profit improvement effort with shared benefits—focused on how to make longer-term commitments with their people.

We started to strike continuously at aspects of silo thinking to get middle-level managers to think more in terms of focused teamwork. These efforts started to bear fruit as gradually we were able to get the mutual, long-term commitments we thought constituted the missing ingredient. Groups that were traditionally hostile or adversarial began to see the shared benefits that could derive from putting aside long-standing confrontational attitudes. Eventually, we were able to extend this technique to suppliers and selected customers, with a surprising amount of success.

The true missing ingredient, we discovered, was the lack of understanding that the continuous improvement process has real meaning for individuals throughout the business network, which includes suppliers of necessary raw materials and outside services; the manufacturing, selling, and administrative organization that creates the finished product or service; and the customers and ultimate end users. Most participants in such a network look at an improvement effort as something that provides more profits for the manufacturing or service firm and recognition for a few leaders; there is little sense of personal gain by employees, managers, suppliers, or customers.

We took this insight into our pilot operations and began to work diligently on building mutual success factors. We tried to get managers out of their silos to discover the wealth of helpful information available to them. The tests we conducted demonstrated that when the silos were left behind and mutual benefit alliances were formed with eager participants, the success rate of improvement ideas climbed dramatically. We found that it was necessary to clearly demonstrate how the benefits would accrue to all who participated in the improvement process.

These tests led to permanent alliances within our organization between formerly adversarial units, which eventually expanded to include suppliers and customers. We were able to get leaders to commit to focused, three-to-five-year improvement strategies with specific commitments and objectives that made as much sense to employees as they did to management. Because of these alliances, leaders had to maintain an orientation to the central objectives, plans, and tactics that had received mutual endorsement. We developed mission statements that bound leaders and followers to courses that clearly benefited the organization, management, employees, suppliers, and customers. It therefore became much easier to override leaders' knee-jerk attempts at quick-fix strategies.

As we broke down the barriers between the silos dotting our business landscape, we found that astonishing improvements to overall performance were possible and that the people involved developed a desire to keep the effort alive. Continuous improvement became more of a reality as silo thinking gave way to concern for long-term organizational success. As middle managers and workers started believing the two-to-three-year commitments given by their oriented leaders, the organizations reached new heights of accomplishment. Organizations that refused to accept this new paradigm in thinking continued to make—or not make—progress at the traditional pace, forever waiting for the occasional spark of individual performance that would, for a moment, create the short-term spurt in productivity so idolized by U.S. management.

Purpose of This Book

Our objective is to present a system that will enhance the ability of suppliers and buyers, manufacturers and sellers, customers and users to create and receive new products and services with consistently improving characteristics. We want to illustrate how to use a new system of techniques to raise annual performances above the average—to new heights of accomplishment in manufacturing, delivery, customer service, and all other areas necessary for survival in today's global competition. Done properly, this system will generate the highest possible quality, the greatest productivity, and consistently high profit and satisfaction from the beginning to the end of a typical business chain.

Our analysis focuses on the logical integration of the better features of available improvement techniques into a complete partnering system with a constant purpose—continuous improvement for mutual benefit. The ultimate result will be the successful implementation of a complete improvement effort that optimizes the use of all resources within an organization.

As we develop our arguments in the ensuing chapters, it will become obvious that we have a deep respect for our Japanese competitors and their ability to draw greater results from their employees as they create a steady stream of quality and productivity innovations. At the same time, we have an unyielding faith in the American worker and his or her ability to meet any challenge under the direction of enlightened leadership. Our experiences lead us to recommend that substantially more enlightened leadership and a far greater degree of partnering are needed. These two factors are the keys to future success, as the Japanese and a few domestic firms have already learned.

Action Study: A Lesson Learned

As we develop our two major themes, we will include action studies that illustrate our points. Our first study describes a personal experience from which we learned firsthand the necessity of overcoming silo thinking. In the late 1970s, Bill Houser was managing, among other things, the quality and service functions for America's largest producer of bicycles. Here is his learning experience.

Our company had introduced a new bicycle at this time and was encountering a significant amount of difficulty. As a responsible manufacturer, we did not ship our mistakes to the customers, so we had avoided what would have been an avalanche of field complaints. We were, however, incuring huge cost variances and schedule delays due to problems inherent in manufacturing this new bicycle.

This particular model was a little out of the ordinary. It was a motocross style with a suspension system built into the frame. Kids loved it, and parents were buying them by the thousands. Stores couldn't keep them in stock. While this should have been music to our ears, because of the difficulties of making the unit, we cringed every time we received an order.

Each time we made a production run of these bicycles the scrap and rework rates would jump dramatically. We certainly pursued improvement but found it was not just a matter of making mechanical changes. A substantial inhibitor to progress was the internal fighting and finger pointing about who deserved the blame for the situation.

The general manager called a meeting with the critical individuals, the managers of Engineering, Production, and Quality, to resolve the situation. It should be recognized that the three summoned parties were good friends and supposedly shared a mutual respect. Unfortunately, this situation was driving a deep wedge between us, and there did not seem to be an acceptable solution at hand. What the general manager realized was that a consensus had to be reached, and it had to derive from the managers most able to create the necessary changes. In our new terminology, we now recognize this leader knew he had to display oriented leadership and to tear down the silos on his property.

My position was clear (of course). Engineering had produced a configuration that was very difficult to build, and the manufacturing processes were not capable of producing the required quality. Obviously, the blame had to be shared by Engineering and Manufacturing.

As absurd as it may sound, both Engineering and Manufacturing disagreed with me (and, with each other). While manufacturing agreed that the Engineering drawings were impossibly difficult for our manufacturing processes, they also thought the quality requirements were too stringent. Engineering agreed that Manufacturing was doing a poor job of managing their process and also believed the quality standards were inappropriate.

In other words, we all knew we were blameless. The fault was with some other function. The ego turfs were preventing a solution critical to organizational success. Our silos were tightly bricked.

The general manager allowed this confrontation to continue for a while. Disappointed by our inability to reach a logical resolution, he then did what oriented leaders have to do. He pointed out that while each of us individually could do little to resolve the issue, collectively we could do practically anything. For example, Engineering could change the configuration, but they could not change the processes or standards. Manufacturing could change the processes, but they could not change the configuration or standards. And Quality could change the standards, but could not change the configuration or processes.

While individually we were limited, collectively we could change the configuration, processes, or standards. For all practical purposes, our only limitation was our collective imagination.

Having made this statement, the general manager charged us with *collectively* solving the problem quickly. He said we would be judged as a group rather than as individuals. We were to come back in two weeks and explain how we had solved the problem. We would *not* be allowed to discuss whose fault it was. He was determined to overcome the personal issues by focusing his subordinates on a mutual solution.

In response to these strong instructions, we proceeded to work together to resolve the difficulties with no thought of whose turf was involved as suggestions were made and discussed. Some of the improvements suggested and accepted involved changing the processes where the processes were not capable of producing acceptable product. In a number of cases the drawings were changed to make more realistic tolerances and correct errors. And it probably comes as no surprise that the standards were corrected (loosened, tightened, or changed) in a number of cases to ensure a quality product.

Needless to say, we collectively discovered how our silos were making us resist what was necessary—a joint improvement effort. When we broke down our silos and began practicing synergy, the numerous problems with the product were solved, and the product went on to be a major success in the marketplace and at the bottom line.

Afterward we tended to use the same partnering process when we had other projects needing our collective attention.

As for the general manager, I would like to think that his insight into human behavior is one of the reasons that Harry Shaw became president and is currently chairman of the board of Huffy Corporation.

Summary

Businesses of all sizes, foreign and domestic, are pursuing some form of improvement process. The more aggressive firms chase stretch goals and are raising the performance levels needed to excel in today's business arena. To operate a company and not pursue continuous improvement against tough objectives is to be left behind these more aggressive competitors. In the current global environment, that situation spells doom. The circumstances for today's businesses translate into two conditions:

- No matter how high the current organizational performance is, any letup in effort will result in loss of position.
- Continuous improvement is a current business imperative and must be pursued with vigor.

Although many firms claim to understand these conditions and have declared themselves to be in the chase, only a few are successful. It is not only necessary to pursue better performance, it is now necessary to achieve great results.

There are many obstacles to organizational improvement processes. The most prevalent is a disoriented leadership that does not stay focused on the correct objectives and does not continue the support necessary to secure successful implementation. Equally destructive is tubular thinking that refuses to accept or to share the help necessary to make quantum jumps forward in progress. What U.S. businesses need is an environment that fosters horizontal interaction to overcome the silo-like separations that dot the landscape of American enterprise.

Partnering appears as the logical catalyst to overcome these obstacles, bind the involved parties, and cause the necessary alliances to coalesce so that significant progress will be secured. For these reasons, business partnering for continuous improvement becomes a strategy for success and endurance in the 1990s and beyond.

Chapter Two

◆

THE CONTINUOUS IMPROVEMENT MODEL

In this chapter, we describe the continuous improvement process, asserting that successful implementation

- Necessitates a three-part effort simultaneously focused on quality, productivity, and profit
- Advances in stages
- Requires a model to guide implementation
- Should be custom-fitted to the circumstances within an organization

The ultimate objective of the continous improvement process is a world-class organization with a distinct competitve advantage. Before discussing the improvement process, let us examine the characteristics of world-class, successful organizations.

Characteristics of Excellent Performers

What do world-class, successful organizations look like? As we assembled our portfolio from the hundred-plus organizations we studied, we paid particular attention to separating real results from intended results. Slowly, as we concentrated on actual achievements, the qualities of excellent performers emerged, and we catalogued those results for both a manufacturing (plant) environment and for an office or service organization (see Tables 2.1 and 2.2). We offer these descriptions as a guide to the reader who wishes to develop an organization-

Table 2.1. Characteristics of a World-Class Plant.

1. Safety	High safety awareness exists day to day. Equipment is properly guarded. All employees are trained in safe practices and consistently wear protective equipment. The work environment is such that zero lost time is a reality. Personal suffering does not exist.
2. Involved and committed workforce	Employees at all levels understand and are committed to making continual improvement through generating ideas, assuming accountability for their work, and actively participating on corrective action teams. Usable suggestions per employee per year approach ten.
3. Just-in-time manufacturing and deliveries to customers	Quality product is manufactured and delivered *when needed*. On-time deliveries exceed 98 percent and approach 100 percent.
4. Focus on product flow	Residence time of material is short. Material moves smoothly from one operation to another.
5. Preventive/predictive maintenance	Machine breakdowns during scheduled run hours are virtually nonexistent. Machines are maintained to run quality product. Delay time is approaching zero on all major operations.
6. Bottlenecks managed	Frequency and severity of bottlenecks, in all areas, have been identified and are appropriately managed. As bottlenecks appear in other areas, they are quickly identified and resolved.
7. Total quality management	Actions at all levels are centered on continually improving the quality of products, processes, and systems. Quality products and services are consistently produced, with results approaching zero defects.
8. Fast setups	Setups are approaching single digits. Because they take such little time, the plant has maximum flexibility to meet customer needs.
9. Extreme low inventories	Raw material, work-in-process, and finished goods inventories are driven down to extremely low levels.
10. Supportive policies/ procedures	Corporate and plant policies and procedures (labor contracts, incentive plans, information reporting, measurement, and so on) support, not hinder, the improvement process.

Table 2.2. Characteristics of a World-Class Service Organization.

1. Accessibility	Employees are available when needed, easily approachable, and customer friendly. Whether contact is in person or by electronic linkage, customers receive the feeling that a responsible person will be accessed during the time of need. Follow-up is performed by the appropriate person(s) in the least possible time, and frequency of contact is matched to need.
2. Competence	Employees have the required skills and knowledge and are proactive in demonstrating those skills to customers. Personnel are experienced and take responsibility for effectively satisfying customers with the highest possible quality. Business is conducted in an organized and professional manner. In-house expertise is available to support the continuous improvement process or to interface with customers.
3. Attitude	Personnel demonstrate a positive and flexible attitude, with a commitment to constantly improve. They are helpful, possess a can-do spirit, act with a sense of urgency for the customer's importance, are courteous, cooperative, and enthusiastic. The customer receives a feeling that problems will get personal care and priority attention.
4. Communication	Employees have an ingrained feeling that the customer should be as well informed as they are, and they strive to transmit all the information necessary to sustain a superior relationship. Changes that affect the business relationship—policies, procedures, organization, new services—are shared with customers.
5. Credibility	Employees demonstrate an aura of believability, integrity, and trustworthiness. The services performed meet the customer requirements as verified by periodic survey checks. Personnel consistently behave in an ethical manner. Business practices inspire trust and confidence.
6. Features/innovation	The firm is on the leading edge in introducing new services that are proactive, customer friendly, and result in higher satisfaction and lower service cycle times. Annual improvements are a part of standard practices.
7. Responsiveness	Employees are characterized by their willingness to provide service to customers. Complaints are resolved quickly and effectively. The customers possess a feeling of fair treatment and thorough resolution to issues or problems. Requests for information are handled in a timely manner.

Table 2.2. Characteristics of a World-Class Service Organization, Cont'd.

8. Tangible results	The firm is noteworthy for physical evidence of service that is documented and disseminated. Effective solutions to specific customer needs can be articulated by all employees. Services provided match the commitments made to the customers. Quality improvement is measured, and recognition is clearly connected to progress.

specific list of world-class characteristics and to those who want to gain a sense of where a global improvement effort is headed. We recommend that these characteristics, or some version developed for a specific organization, be used to define the end result of a successful continuous improvement effort. In that way, a focused orientation can be developed, with specific targeted characteristics. It is only when an operation approaches these performance levels that continuous improvement becomes a part of the business system and a competitive advantage is attained.

Linking Quality, Productivity, and Profit Improvement

There are three equally critical ingredients for business success: quality, productivity, and profit improvement. We recognize that arguments can be advanced for pursuing a singular-focus improvement process, with quality being the current favorite. A review of the literature in the quality category reveals, however, that many leading authorities espouse the interconnection of quality with other improvement categories. One of our favorite quotations by the foremost expert on quality, W. Edwards Deming (1982, p. 1), reflects this multiple emphasis. He states, "As quality increases, productivity increases. This fact is well known, but only to a select few." Deming has steadfastly argued the importance of the quality ethic, but he has been equally clear that such an orientation brings positive results in productivity and profits.

Armand Feigenbaum (1991, p. 20) further establishes the connection. In the fortieth anniversary edition of his book *Total Quality Control,* he discusses how managing the cost of quality control (his central improvement theme) will have a major impact on each of the factors he believes influences profitability: "Through careful analysis of customer wants and needs, the product can be provided with those qualities which motivate purchase by the customer and thus increase salability. When the quality of the product design and production process is established with producibility in mind, manufacturing costs can be substantially reduced and the possibility minimized of negative cost offsets. . . . With the balanced manufacturing capability for quality production in place, productivity rises as cost per unit decreases."

We argue that these three elements of a business—quality, productivity, and profit improvement—are too closely interrelated not to be considered coequal parts of an improvement effort. If the ultimate business objective is to sustain a competitive advantage, attaining that position requires superior performance in all three areas. Advantage accrues because customers want to give orders to an organization whose employees create and deliver outstanding quality, at competitive costs, so productively that satisfaction is ensured. In succinct terms, a world-class firm wants to "delight" the customer with the highest quality goods and services at a fair price and to make a reasonable profit to cover survival, stockholder, and reinvestment requirements. The customer receives quality when required in the quantities necessary without delay or unnecessary inventories, is serviced reliably, and receives a competitive price, while the alliances formed as part of the business arrangement seek further savings. The organization's suppliers perform to these same high standards and make a profit, so they remain in existence to provide those standards in the future.

These requirements necessitate a complete improvement process. Quality can be the central feature of the effort, but denying the need to raise productivity and improve profitability simultaneously is to deny the obvious. To illustrate our point, imagine a near-to-life story that begins about a decade ago. In this situation, we witness how a motivated leader with seemingly dedicated subordinates can become disappointed by a well-intentioned false start—one with a single improvement focus.

Alice's Dilemma

Alice Harper was a manager on the move. She had progressed quickly through a series of promotions that spanned staff marketing positions and direct sales assignments. Now she was the general manager responsible for running a converting operation that made a finished consumer product from material supplied primarily by the parent company—an integrated metal fabricating firm. There were six such operations within the firm, characterized by a fair amount of professional jealousy over which was the best performer of the group.

Following a brief orientation period in her new job, Alice found that her unit had a long history of making profits, ranging from 2 to 7.5 percent of net sales. The quality reputation for the basic product line was considered fair-to-good by internal and external surveys—a 6.8 on a 1–10 scale. The five-year plan called for her to make a 5 percent annualized improvement to earnings. All raw material consumed was to be from factories owned by the parent company.

One day, while reading an industry trade journal, she noticed an article that described how a quality expert had been retained by a major competitor. This competitor, it was claimed, had achieved a significant improvement to quality by applying techniques explained by the expert. The competition had also improved earnings by 20 percent over a two-year period.

Impressed by this story, Alice contacted the expert and arranged a presentation for her immediate reports. During this presentation, the quality expert outlined a thirteen-step process that would lead to con-

sistent high quality and bring substantial cost reductions. At the conclusion of this meeting, Alice and her direct-reporting managers agreed to embark on the recommended process—immediately. Their collective conclusion was that this process would enable them to beat the volume and earnings budget for their business unit and to surpass the other units in the group.

Alice and her managers were taken to a local sound studio, where Alice taped an enthusiastic endorsement of what was to be called the Quality and Work Improvement Process (QWIP). The managers each filmed a portion of the thirteen-step procedure, explaining what the steps meant and how they were to be executed. The tape ended with an exhortation from Alice to "make it happen, for the good of all of us who work at this plant."

A special day was selected for showing this tape to all employees. A meal was catered, local dignitaries were invited to attend, a senior official from the parent company delivered an inspirational speech, and the tape was shown. All employees were asked to sign a statement of commitment, following the tape viewing, that they would make quality happen by giving their best performance—all the time.

During the first six months after that special day, productivity went up 15 percent and returns and allowances went down 20 percent. A follow-up Appreciation Day was held and a small gift given to all employees. Alice and her managers agreed the process was "generally working."

The year-end audit, conducted for all converting operations, confounded their assessment. The "general findings" included the following:

- Although R&A (returns and allowances) was down 10 percent, waste had increased by three points. Savings from R&A amounted to $50,000; the increased waste had cost $212,000.
- A check of the production reports indicated efficiency data were suspect because of invalid entries in three major departments.
- Although a special commendation had been received from their largest customer naming the plant as the "quality supplier of the year," six lesser accounts had canceled orders. Their collective reason: deteriorating attention to quality.

- *Two key department supervisors resigned, citing total lack of management support as their reason for leaving.*
- *Of greater concern to Alice's boss and members of the parent company's executive committee, earnings were down 12 percent.*

Personal interviews with some of the employees and managers also provided interesting comments:

A Line Supervisor (at the exit interview):

"Sure I let my people put down bad production entries. Management was looking for an increase in efficiency, so I gave it to them. If I didn't, they probably would have taken people away from me. And I need everybody I got! Right in the middle of the new process we put in a new machine. Nobody knew how to run it . . . and I was going to risk losing the operators I had? No way!"

A Line Supervisor:

"This quality thing is a good idea. It got everybody excited, but all it did for me was make more problems. I'm not supposed to put any bad material through my presses, so I send the bad stuff to the scrap area. Now I have to shut down machines because we don't have enough material and our costs are going up instead of down. We were supposed to get our suppliers in line. I guess that didn't include our own mills."

Quality Control Manager:

"The system will work, if we just have enough patience, but I don't see it happening for two, maybe three years. If I took my inspectors off now, we would go out of business."

Customer Service Manager:

"When we first started, I became very enthused. I told our customers that quality was going to be the number one priority. They could forget about bad units, get rid of incoming inspection. Now they laugh at me every time there is a problem. I'm tired of having my nose rubbed in it. I don't even talk quality any more."

Sales Representative:

"I knew it would not happen, when Alice told us about it. We never did have good quality and nothing has changed. I spend half my time convincing my customers to use that crap we make. If it wasn't for my relationships, we would have lost every piece of business I brought in here."

Accounting Manager:

"They told us to keep track of errors. That way, we were supposed to find ways to do things right. So we did just that. At first, we learned how to clean up a few problems, but we never changed the systems that caused the problems in the first place. Now if we list errors, they say we don't know how to do our jobs. I told my people to forget about it. The month-end closing is all they care about, anyhow."

Production Manager:

"Alice is trying hard. We should all support her program. She just doesn't know enough about manufacturing. With what we have to work with, we're doing a good job. I told her to ease off a little and give it more time. We were on the right track any way. Once the new machine gets cranking, we'll make the targets."

Sales Manager:

"I just did not understand what we were agreeing to do. It all sounded so good—and so simple. All we had to do was start doing things right. When I said I was committed, I meant it. But I didn't realize what I had to do. Like when they told me Dave Henrickes (the top sales representative) was not cooperating. I never expected my commitment meant I had to put him on notice. Now really! He carries so much business!"

When Alice called her boss to discuss the lack of progress and relayed some of these comments, the response was curt: "Then you have to get the people who will make it happen. Your job is on the line here, Alice."

Alice faces a real—and unfortunately very typical—dilemma. In spite of very good intentions, her business unit was not prepared for a commitment to a single-focus process with such lofty ambitions. This situation is regrettable because her managers, her people, and her firm would all have done better if the process she tried to implement had succeeded. Financial gains could have been made at many levels. Customer satisfaction would have increased. Job security would be better. Unfortunately, good intentions and a good focus do not guarantee success. In Alice's case, the results she sought are eluding her. She is confused as she faces a career dilemma.

Continuous Improvement: Three Levels of Progression

Were we to advise our heroine, we would start with a discussion of the limitations of Alice Harper's reliance on a thirteen-step process. We would try to convince her of the folly of expecting world-class results without making a long-term commitment to improvement in the three areas crucial to business success, and to prepare her for the inevitable declines she must encounter and overcome. With her understanding of the real task before her, we would then detail what our extensive study of improvement efforts has revealed: there are distinct levels of progression associated with attaining continuous improvement, and the truly successful improvement efforts in business evolve through these stages:

Level 1: Dedication

- Management (particularly at senior levels) becomes excited about establishing a process through which quality and efficiency will improve. At the center of this enthusiasm is a belief that costs will decline, customer satisfaction will rise, and the organization will be a better place in which to work.
- Policy deployment—the term used to describe the selection of issues and objectives on which to concentrate the improvement effort—is top-down. Team problem solving is encouraged, usually in some stepped procedure under the direction of a trained facilitator.
- Communication systems are established to publicize the process and the success stories. The CEO and a few senior executives are captured on film extolling the importance and the virtue of the improvement process. Middle management is generally left with the task of securing implementation, and front-line supervisors have the bulk of responsibility for encouraging the required actions.
- The life cycle for Level 1 is about eighteen months. The demise is quiet. The mourning is minimal. There is no

official funeral. The process simply falls into disuse because the leaders direct their attention elsewhere and the
middle managers go back to business as usual.

Level 2: Sustenance

- Organizations that fail at Level 1 find they have to repeat
  the process if they want to achieve success. Those that
  pass to Level 2 do so because they recognize the many
  barriers to sustaining the process and refuse to let the
  spark that incited the effort expire. These organizations
  sustain their orientation to continuous improvement but
  work harder at finding the issues and opportunities that
  have meaning across the entire organization.
- Management continues to select the improvement initiatives. But because of a belief in the ability of workers to
  contribute, the formation of action teams has become a
  standard procedure. When an issue is identified, action
  teams are quickly formed to seek resolution. Training in
  the formation of teams and how they should function to
  solve problems has been conducted for hourly and salaried personnel, and people are ready and willing to share
  their ideas. Teams are cross-functional and have both employee and management representation.
- Weaknesses in systems and procedures, including how
  rewards, promotions, information, and criticism are handled, are identified and improvement efforts begun.
- Training becomes a major factor in Level 2; employees
  begin identifying their own areas of need, rather than
  waiting on management to do so.
- Communications are much more open, and traditionally
  closed areas are exposed to a more interested and contributing workforce.

Level 3: Continuity

- The improvement process has become institutionalized.
  Policy deployment moves in both directions, and man-

agement's role entails far more counseling and coaching of employees than was previously the case.

- The need for training is no longer questioned, and training is not done on a payback basis. It is simply done in all areas.
- Idea generation climbs to unprecedented heights, reaching five to ten (or more) usable suggestions per employee per year. These ideas reflect the original dedication to quality and customer satisfaction and are quickly turned into team actions.
- The data and information necessary to improve the organization are gathered and analyzed by the workers, who then recommend sensible changes.
- Those within the organization—individuals, teams, departments, and sites—who contribute to its success are clearly recognized and rewarded.

Level 1

At Level 1, some inspirational message is passed on by a high authority, and an edict is issued that the process embodied within that message be implemented. During this stage, much enthusiasm, training, support materials, and meeting time are devoted to the effort. Oversight committees come into existence, apparel bearing the process acronym appears throughout the organization, action teams are formed, and some early successes are achieved and publicized. Involvement of non-salaried employees might be tested, but usually Level 1 is a management exercise that shows strong support for an improvement process that is poorly understood and more poorly executed.

Why do organizations fail to move on to Level 2? Problems start with the withdrawal of senior level support, are compounded by the lack of middle management understanding of how to really implement the process, and finally end with the failure to move the process into the hands of the people who are the true executors of all improvements: the rank-and-file and support employees. The process stagnates because too many managers and first-line supervisors believe the improvement has been achieved. Our interviews with hundreds of these individuals have shown us that they took a short-term view of the effort and concluded that the job was finished as soon as they had some identifiable results. After all, the process had ten, twelve, or fourteen steps, each of which was executed. The sequence was more or less followed. The few successes were noted and perhaps even rewarded. These implementors found they were left on their own to consider what should be done next. Without directives to recycle or explanations of how to achieve more progress, there was little incentive to continue the process.

For most organizations, the dedication to successful implementation is not cleanly dropped. It is sustained in some lukewarm fashion until a crossroad is reached, when people throughout the organization or unit watch intently to see how leadership will react. When the tenets of the improvement process are violated at that "moment of crisis," the implementation goes into decline.

Level 2

Some organizations are able to sustain the effort and continue on to Level 2. The leading quality consultants, for example, all have clients who persisted until some success was achieved. Unfortunately, many organizations end up with islands of success instead of enjoying companywide implementation. The improvement process occurs in those sectors that most need and want the type of help provided by that particular process. Other sectors often ignore the designated process and conduct their own version of improvement.

The companies that make the transition to Level 2 negotiate the "moment of crisis" and signal throughout the organization that the process will not be allowed to die. The ideas and the necessary improvements are enacted. When the choice is quality or profit-for-the-moment, the decision goes with quality. The favoring of quality becomes very important for those within the firm, and a sense of pride begins to germinate. Champions appear throughout the company, who foster the right way to do things rather than short-term, politically correct actions.

Silo structures are dismantled in Level 2 so inter- and intraorganizational synergies become a reality, not a myth. Employee involvement increases as team problem solving expands throughout the organization. Teams include salaried, hourly, line, support, technical, and nontechnical employees. From the CEO to the newest employee, the thrust of the improvement process is constantly reinforced. Rather than settling for islands of success, an attempt is made for companywide improvement. No one concept predominates, but the best of all ideas are applied to specific situations that demand improvement. A momentum develops that defeats the usual cultural inertia, and the process begins to be ingrained in how things are accomplished.

At Level 2, messengers are not killed, and when the emperor shows up without clothes, people advise their leader to get dressed. Dissent is encouraged instead of suppressed. Leaders are not afraid to admit shortcomings of their organizations. Rather, they encourage identification of the real opportunities to change what has been happening for too long.

Some firms resist behaving like a Level 2 organization until they are forced into it by an important customer who insists on partnering only with organizations demonstrating the characteristics of Level 2. That circumstance is the worst way to move to Level 2. There is no true dedication. The effort becomes an exercise focused on satisfying that particular customer. Management feigns endorsement, and employees pretend to implement.

The key to Level 2 is total commitment to and full involvement in an understood process of continuous improvement.

Policy can be deployed downward in the traditional manner. Management can spell out the major issues and objectives. But action teams are formed quickly because the workers know how to and want to mobilize corrective action. Cultural barriers are easily overcome. Tradition gives way to effort that generates progress. Lots of empowered people are focused on quality, customer satisfaction, productivity, and cost improvement in a holistic manner. The organization and its stakeholders are moving toward continuous improvement, competitive advantage, and long-term stability.

Level 3

A few organizations pass into Level 3. At this level, policy is deployed upward as well as downward. People at all levels of the organization contribute concepts and ideas (ten to thirty per person per year) on how the complete improvement process can move to higher stages of improvement. Leadership at this level is active and visibly involved throughout the firm. The firm can now extend what has been learned and achieved outside of the organization without fear of failure. Florida Power and Light, one of the leading Level 3 organizations, now offers the features of their process on a consulting basis.

Level 3 is an interesting environment. Cooperative effort is so strong that everyone is involved in customer satisfaction and the selling process. Training is extensive, and skills move forward without regard for the cost of training. Motorola reports they spend about 2.5 percent of the payroll cost on training without requiring payback data (Hooker, 1991). They do it because "it is the right thing to do." Rewards and recognition are second nature, as the entire organization thrives on documented progress. Accounting and control have moved to a higher, proactive state, wherein all measurement is by facts, generated by those who perform the function. Activity-based accounting, user friendly and helpful information systems, and all support department activities assist the improvement process. There is a constancy of purpose behind the process that enables people to know their focus will not be changed just as they start to make progress.

When an organization finds itself on the threshold of Level 3, either at particular locations or throughout a division or the entire firm, it is ready to employ the concept of partnering (defined and explained more fully in Chapter Three). Our recommendation is to begin internally first, to form alliances with all employees in order to strengthen the team effort and to create a greater sense that the effort will be sustained. Next, the movement should be toward external partnering—first with suppliers, and then with customers.

Alice and her managers thought they could apply a prescriptive type of improvement process and leap into Level 3–type success. It simply cannot be done! The reality of Alice's situation is that she is bogged down in Level 1; she must search for something that will unite her organization, with all employees seeing mutual advantages for cooperating. We will leave Alice temporarily to consider how she could orient her leadership toward something with greater meaning than the enactment of a lockstep procedure. We move now to explain our continuous improvement model and discuss how to begin a continuous improvement process.

The Continuous Improvement Model

The continuous improvement model consists of three major components (represented by the three rings in Figure 2.1) that must operate as a consistent system to be effective. Our model posits a three-phase effort, beginning with the analysis pictured in the outer ring of Figure 2.1, moving through the middle level, and finally focusing on the elements in the inner ring.

To begin an improvement effort, it is necessary to first analyze current organizational conditions to identify how improvement can logically be interwoven with local systems and procedures to ensure successful implementation. The outer

Figure 2.1. The Continuous Improvement Model.

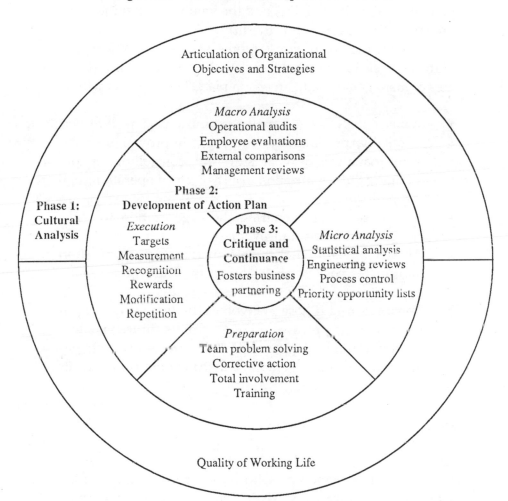

Articulation of Organizational
Objectives and Strategies

Macro Analysis
Operational audits
Employee evaluations
External comparisons
Management reviews

Phase 2:
Development of Action Plan

Phase 1:
Cultural
Analysis

Execution
Targets
Measurement
Recognition
Rewards
Modification
Repetition

Phase 3:
**Critique and
Continuance**
Fosters business
partnering

Micro Analysis
Statistical analysis
Engineering reviews
Process control
Priority opportunity lists

Preparation
Team problem solving
Corrective action
Total involvement
Training

Quality of Working Life

ring (Phase 1) is primarily cultural and represents the need
to combine the central purposes and values of the organization
with the intentions of the improvement process. The ring is
divided into two sections. The first section depicts the objectives and strategies articulated by senior management as they
seek to raise productivity and quality and improve profits—
the three-part focus so necessary for success. The second part

of the ring shows the organization's stance with respect to people, quality of work life, and the value of individuals and group participation within the firm.

The middle ring (Phase 2) represents the four critical parts of the analysis process that translate the objectives and strategies of management into an action plan. These parts include:

- A macroanalysis of where the organization is with respect to quality, productivity, and profit improvement
- A microanalysis of what is driving, controlling, or constraining the organization in all aspects of operations and job performance
- A procedure for preparing the organization to make planned, targeted improvements
- An execution format that maximizes the synergistic effort and creates positive results across the entire organization

The inner ring (Phase 3) involves the two factors necessary to sustain the process and to ensure its future viability: an honest and frank critique of how the process is progressing and a set of implementation instructions to ensure its continuance.

Phase 1: Cultural Analysis

An improvement effort should start with a preliminary assessment and understanding of how the process will function within the organization's existing cultural framework. What is being initiated should not impose contradictory values on the personnel involved; it is much better to build the new values within the framework of the existing culture than to impose dramatic change. If an organization needs changing for survival and growth purposes, the continuous improvement process will yield those changes as positive results are achieved. If time is a luxury that cannot be afforded, management should introduce the necessary changes, allow time for assimilation, and then embark on an improvement process with the revised organization.

Articulation of Organizational Objectives and Strategies. This first assessment reviews exactly what senior management wants to accomplish and how productivity, quality, and profit improvement will become the critical three parts of the accomplishment strategy. An important factor at this stage is that as objectives are articulated, they must include all parts of the organization. If this requirement is not met, the effort is doomed to be a short-term program, most likely focused on reducing manufacturing costs and overhead.

It is critical that those who guide the improvement process be aware of existing cultural constraints. If sales, for example, is a sacred area and not subject to improvement review, we can guarantee that order entry will never reach world-class standards. If engineering is exempt from critical review, finished products will never fully satisfy the customer. Often a planned improvement effort is enthusiastically launched, but implementation stagnates because those responsible for profit and loss reach critical crossroads and fail to execute on the intended purposes. In retrospect, these managers find they were confronted with decisions where prevailing practices or cultural inhibitors contradicted the tenets of the new system.

A simple example is the manager who faces the perplexing problem of whether or not to scrap a large order because of off-specification quality. Traditionally, the emphasis (or cultural pressure) would be on getting the customer to use the product rather than incur the short-term negative impact to earnings. Conversely, the new quality plan is to ship no product that is not totally within specification. At this crossroad, the perplexed manager must decide between a new purpose and the cultural imperative. The problem is that without clear executive articulation, decisions will vary, creating vast differences between business units. This lack of consistency will drastically subtract from results and confuse participants.

Quality of Working Life. The other factors to consider from a cultural perspective are the degree of importance the organization attaches to the role of people and the objectives management wants to pursue in terms of quality of working life. The most successful improvement efforts invariably include a strong orientation toward the people aspects of the system they foster.

Underlying the pursuit of continuous improvement is one central concept: *At all times, all parts of the organization are seeking the best that can be achieved in all aspects of job performance.* Contained within this concept is the necessity to critically evaluate all elements of the process, especially the people factors. When the element of cost is related to people, for example, the primary objective must be to keep the organization prime (so as not to incur extra burden) without jeopardizing its future potential. This statement translates into "rightsizing"—maintaining the correct collection of high-caliber managers and subordinates to accomplish today's targets and to build for tomorrow's challenges.

At the same time, the work load must be consistently managed so that redundancy, inappropriateness, obsolescence, and other personally debilitating factors do not enter the picture. The work load has to be kept as prime as the number of employees; if it is not, the firm will fail to optimize performance. When performance is optimized and benefits derived, it is strongly recommended that a portion of those benefits be shared with the people who contributed to the accomplishment.

Quality of working life involves the prevailing attitude the organization has toward the role of all personnel—their value as individuals and their contributions to the firm. Unless there is as much dedication to the future value of employees as to keeping the organization trim, there is no need for the type of three-part strategy being proposed. It will suffice to have periodic cost reduction programs or to apply significant annual capital expenditures toward the maximum possible automation.

One important output of the cultural portion of the model should be a specific articulation by the CEO that details the purpose, scope, and constituent elements of the improvement strategy. Inherent in that message is a mission statement that reflects management posture with respect to the elements of financial expectations, job performance, value of employees, necessary achievements, customer orientation, and organizational responsibilities. Quality, productivity, and profit improvement should not be obscure concepts; they should be integrated within the statement as basic parts of an ongoing change process that eventually becomes normal business activity.

Phase 2: Development of Action Plan

Macro- and Microanalyses. Once the cultural and executive imperatives have been documented in a mission statement, the macroanalysis—examining where the organization is, where it wants to go, and what people think it will take to get there—should be started.

This macroanalysis should be performed from both an internal and external viewpoint. (In Chapter Five, we describe one of our favorite techniques—an operational analysis conducted with a joint internal/external team.) Internally, some form of operational audit, employee evaluation, or management overview should be conducted on each part of the organization. With the information gathered from such an audit, evaluations against outside benchmarks of industry norms should be used to establish stretch measures of competitive performance. Progress to an improved position has to begin with a solid understanding of where the business is starting—internally and externally. More demands should be placed on those units that compare dismally with their peers than on ones that are setting the industry standard.

The review phase should turn next to the specific areas highlighted by the macro-overview. If the larger analysis, for example, shows a significant gap between desired and actual performance in a certain area of the organization, the logical next step is to conduct a microanalysis. Now a closer look is given to the particular area of concern to determine what the real issues or problems are, what drives the inherent processes, and where the opportunities are for improvement. In this phase, those conducting the improvement program should involve as many employees as appropriate and encourage the following:

- Use of statistical analysis and review to establish the control points in the process or procedure
- Development of Pareto charts to isolate the higher-priority issues, opportunities, and problems
- Use of industrial engineering techniques to propose potential improvements to methods, systems, and procedures
- Use of process control reviews to determine where manual or automatic control techniques can be used to maintain process consistency
- Isolation of the candidate projects for team processing

The guiding philosophy must be that nothing is sacrosanct. There can be no sacred cows as a microanalysis challenges the status quo in the interest of making improvements. Senior management can guide the review teams to specific areas needing improvement, but the teams must be encouraged to look for themselves into all matters that could lead to better performance. That means policy deployment should be started in a top-down manner, but as good results are achieved, a bottom-up phase should be encouraged.

Preparation and Execution. At this point, those conducting the improvement process begin serious preparation for the implementation of the ideas and recommendations generated by the action teams. Several crucial conditions must be in place to ensure success:

- The integration of productivity, quality, and cost improvement has been clearly defined and understood.
- A commitment to improvement has been made by management and related to specific targets throughout the organization.
- The commitment and improvement procedures have been fully explained to all employees.
- Selected individuals have been trained to facilitate the team processing that will take place.
- Problem-solving training has been extensively conducted to prepare employees for team processing.
- Corrective action teams have been formed to work on the resolution of high-priority issues, opportunities, and problems.
- A format has been established to ensure that the maximum possible participation is attained, feedback is real and continuous, and progress is constantly monitored and reported.

If the previous steps have been successfully accomplished, the execution phase moves easily toward accomplishment. At the start of this part of the effort, the process has been reviewed with all employees, the various business units have personnel trained to facilitate team actions, problem-solving techniques are understood, and a prioritized "starter list" of issues, opportunities, and problems is available to initiate action. The remaining steps consist of:

- Establishing appropriate methods for recognizing and rewarding improvements to performance
- Providing the necessary resources to the action teams
- Setting stretch targets that are reasonable and challenging
- Initiating the first action team processing
- Modifying the procedures and techniques to make them more effective
- Rewarding all participants

* Repeating the procedures on the next list of prioritized issues, opportunities, and problems

In Chapter Five, we present the customized model for matching the correct execution tools against the required improvements.

Phase 3: Critique and Continuance. Phase 3 is based on two fundamental propositions: critiquing is a valuable tool for improving performance, and a process requires a planned procedure to ensure its continuance.

Critiquing requires managers and facilitators to objectively review current performance, the action teams, and results achieved. Done properly, a critique isolates the elements that encouraged success and those that inhibited it. Such review should be followed by changes and improvements to lead to even greater effectiveness.

Continuance of the improvement process requires management to squarely face five issues:

1. How can a procedure be established to bring poor performers up to the level of the high achievers?
2. How can the attitude demonstrated by some individuals that "this too shall pass" be overcome?
3. How can the beliefs of the process be built into the existing culture?
4. How should new issues for the action teams be generated?
5. How should the process be tied into the establishment of annualized improvements?

The answers to these questions—and the procedural changes they engender—have to be gathered over a series of honest evaluation sessions. During these sessions, the questions should be squarely addressed, with no recriminations for frank responses. Only by objectively and openly discussing what is being done both correctly and incorrectly, by encouraging the maximum synergistic participation, and by insisting that the process be followed throughout the organization will the improvement effort continue and succeed.

It is during Phase 3 that business partnering intersects with continuous improvement. As the critical review and drive for continuance are pursued, the necessity of building alliances around the positive aspects of those efforts starts to come into focus. From the critique, an honest evaluation of performance points out the problems that can be addressed with appropriate alliances. For example, if sales and production are causing delays or impeding satisfaction, an obvious opportunity for partnering is isolated. As continuance issues are faced, inhibiting attitudes appear that partnering efforts will be able to overcome. Within this inner circle of the model, the realization occurs that the missing ingredient to make the total model work is the forging of alliances.

Action Study: AMEX Life Assurance

For many years AMEX Life Assurance was a successful life insurance organization as part of the Fireman's Fund, a firm that was acquired by American Express in 1968. American Express sold Fireman's Fund in 1986 but elected to retain Fireman's Fund American Life, which eventually changed its name to AMEX Life. Although AMEX Life's profitability was sound, it was characterized by high marketing and management expenses and a limited product portfolio sold through a direct mail system. Neither American Express nor AMEX Life was exactly sure how the insurance carrier complemented the corporate concept of adding value to the customer—the cardholders of American Express.

In 1988—in this environment of uncertainty—AMEX Life set out to find an identity that was compatible with the corporate mission and to transform itself into a customer-oriented financial services firm. Attaining a customer focus was embraced as the key strategy in achieving the desired new state.

The story of AMEX Life's endeavor illustrates how a multifaceted change effort, focused on liberating and harnessing employee creativity and with quality as a central feature, can be enacted. This group progressed to a higher level of success faster than most organizations we have studied. They did so by following a consistently "oriented" leadership and by tearing down all of the typical inhibitions that characterize silo managers. They also expanded beyond the quality imperative to work on features of productivity and cost, as they focused on "customer satisfaction at a profit to the firm." It was a four-year process, but their success demonstrates what can be achieved when the proper dedication, sustenance, and continuity are applied to an improvement effort.

Realizing that an enemy could very well be their own past successes, an early decision was made to attack the concept that everyone in the organization knew they were doing the right things. In our terminology, that meant the effort tried to eliminate any traditional barriers that could foster silo thinking. In 1988, Sarah M. Nolan was made president of the company developing this value-oriented and people-centered culture—the Investments and Insurance Services Group (IISG). Nolan started the new approach by asking a small group of employees to plan the new venture in an office near the central headquarters. These individuals became known as the "Pioneer Group." She explained that their mission was to start a parallel business, from scratch. They would do this by throwing away all of their preconceived ideas and developing a new and improved way to operate a financial services company.

The quality strategy was defined as the group decided that these elements had to be included in the way IISG conducted business:

- Everyone had to talk to customers.
- IISG would create distinctive, customer friendly financial products.
- Superior quality services would be engineered into those products.

The production strategy was also defined:

- The cultural process through which the products would be delivered had to be reengineered.
- IISG would create new habits and thought patterns to positively affect what everyone would do on a daily basis and how employees would define good performance.

- Overall business goals would be integrated into organizational priorities, with both team and personal goals.

The Pioneer team's confidence and belief in people were expressed in these mandates:

- Create empowered teams.
- Create enriched jobs.
- Create a strong customer focus and pride of ownership in the new culture.

This new venture was subsequently integrated into the main office in 1990. The Pioneer group led the way in creating employee teams that now include 60 percent of all IISG employees. Most of the basic strategies remain in effect, and the unit has successfully surpassed the goals set for it. Some features are worthy of note. Rather than perpetuate a typical manager-heavy hierarchical structure, teams conduct all the functions necessary to provide the products and service the customers. Supervisor levels are gone, so only one layer of employees stands between customer and the group director. In fact, the company has 45 percent fewer managers. Activities normally associated with midlevel managers have become a part of the teams' daily activities. Setting work priorities, managing fluctuating business volumes, preparing reports, handling conflicts, and assessing performance are managed by the team members. Quality and productivity improvement have been driven directly into the hands of those who provide the desired service to the customer.

Evelyn Carney, one of the Pioneer team members and now a director of a six-team group, explains some of the new thinking: "The way we run our department is by thinking of ourselves as a small business, where we do everything associated with running the business. Before we went into teams, we were very functionalized. One person would do nothing but card billing. Even if that person were here for ten years, that's what he or she did—card billing. Today, the associates do everything. Of course, we've upgraded the positions and done months of training, but we also have far fewer people doing even more work."

Productivity obviously improved, for fewer people accomplish more work. In most organizations, such a situation would have led to a backlash as the employees tried to pace themselves to a lower level of output. At IISG, Carney explains that the employees went to other achievements: "Teams are self-managed. They decide when to put in extra hours on a weekend, because they know what their workload is. When marketing is planning a solicitation, our marketing people train the entire group on product differences, answers to customer questions, and so on."

In 1989, the Life and Health Customer Service Department had five supervisors and fifty customer service representatives in five functional areas. The department evolved to six teams of five associates, plus a seventh team handling the Canadian market. Typical of the new IISG culture, these teams manage their workloads, set priorities, conduct peer assignments, track team performance, and continually seek ways to improve service to customers. The teams have achieved impressive gains in productivity, quality, and the cost of doing their business. Similar improvements have been noted in employee attendance, customer responsiveness, and correspondence inventory. IISG has proven that a major change and improvement effort can succeed. We believe their story illustrates how a multifaceted, oriented focus can progress, with continued support, to Level 2 of progress (sustenance). More time is needed to see if they move to Level 3 (continuity). For now, they have developed their own model of excellence and pursued it with a consistent orientation, garnering impressive results for their effort.

Summary

There is no profit panacea for business leaders, but there is continuous improvement, which can lead to an organization with world-class status and a sustained competitive advantage. Continuous improvement is an integrated system that requires that quality, productivity, and profit improvement be combined into a single strategy.

American business cannot rely on favorable market conditions to achieve new heights of performance. Organizations must rely on internally generated, continuous progress. Goldratt and Fox (1986, p. 14) conclude: "It is no longer a question of a cycle of good times and bad. We cannot button down the hatches and hope to survive, as if this were another passing storm. We can no longer use the conventional approach of cutting expenses and firing people in the bad times. We must find a way to continually improve—in good times and bad. We must choose to be in the competitive edge race. The companies that elect to shrink in order to pass the bad times will disappear. The ones that survive will be those companies that will find a way to participate in the ever-increasing competitive edge race."

To help win that race, we espouse chasing quality, productivity, and profit improvement simultaneously, on a continuous basis, throughout the full spectrum of the organization.

Chapter Three

◆

THE BUSINESS PARTNERING PROCESS

In the last chapter, we illustrated our continuous improvement model, arguing that competitive advantage is achieved as organizations focus on a three-part improvement effort. In this chapter, we discuss our second theme: business partnering—the building of alliances for mutual benefit throughout an organization's business network. Business partnering is crucial, and we believe it is the key for successful, enduring improvement efforts. To help bring meaning to the concept, let us first revisit Alice Harper and her managers as they attempt to recover from an abortive attempt to implement a single-focus improvement strategy.

Alice Tries Again

It had taken Alice Harper eighteen months to realize that the thirteen-step improvement process her business unit had adopted had failed to achieve its purpose. In spite of early successes, later results all reflected lower levels of performance. Morale fell to unusually low levels, and customer dissatisfaction, as measured by a credible survey company, rose.

Alice decided to scrap the thirteen-step process and exhorted her subordinates to try again to achieve more positive results. The assignment was to help resuscitate the dying improvement effort, reverse all negative performance trends, and increase profits by 15–20 percent. The first step was the formation of a Quality Council. This move was deemed necessary to make sure the new effort, termed a Total Quality Management (TQM) process, would endure. The instructions to the members of the Council were straightforward and simple: "You are to see that we execute," Alice proclaimed. "I know you're committed. Now I want to see action. And I don't want the effort to disappear in a year. We're in this for good! I want us to be recognized as the leading quality supplier in our market, and TQM will do that for us."

The Production Manager had been selected as the Council director, and his first action was to convene a meeting to establish the format and objective of the organization. Other attendees at this session included:

- Quality Control Manager
- Customer Service Manager
- Manufacturing Services Manager
- Sales Manager
- Accounting Manager

After the Production Manager had reviewed the charter set forth by Alice and suggested the group start with a little brainstorming, the Manufacturing Services Manager opened the general discussion.

"You know," he commented with a sigh, "my people are really confused. First it was quality circles. Then it was statistical process control, good old SPC. Then it was thirteen steps to total quality awareness. That was supposed to solve all our problems. Ha! What a laugh! Now Alice says she wants more results on quality. We're supposed to chase something called TQM. We also have to make more money. We can't let up on our cost-reduction targets. When are we going to have one consistent signal?"

The Sales Manager said in a jesting tone, "We get paid for performance around here . . . and that means however the boss defines performance."

The Manufacturing Services Manager dropped a pencil on the table and smirked at the Sales Manager. "I'm getting too old to care. I'm vested, and I've got two or three years before I say good-bye." Turning to the Production Manager, he continued. "The problem is we never see one idea all the way through. We're forever changing the signals we give out. My people say the only thing they can count on is inconsistency from the top. I will gladly give what I can, but for Pete's sake, can't they make up their minds?"

The Production Manager tapped a pencil on the conference room table. "Look, folks, we have to come up with something. If there is confusion out there, our job is to make it go away. That's what we get paid for. Now I think we should start trying to figure out what to do, without crying over things we can't change."

"OK, I'll start," the Accounting Manager said. "It's dollars they are after the most. That's what's behind everything we do. Alice wants us to double our earnings. What we need to do is develop a cost-reduction program and cut out the fat."

"They want more than that," the Quality Control Manager argued. "We'd be stupid to back down from the improvements we've made in quality. If we let people think we're giving up on quality, it will cost us more money. We're far from done. We have to keep the quality effort alive, somehow work it into cost reduction."

"Don't forget the JIT [just-in-time] program. We're just starting to get that going," the Production Manager added. "And I can see a lot coming to the bottom line from that effort. I know it can save us big dollars."

"I've got several of my big customers excited about it," the Sales Manager added. "They can't wait for us to start delivering just what they need . . . on time."

"And SPC," said the Quality Control Manager. "Don't forget all we poured into that. We know it can save us money. That has to be our tool for success. We have all those people trained to do it. All they need to be told is where to focus their attention."

The Production Manager got up and walked to the chart pad at the front of the room. "Suppose we try something like this," he remarked while selecting a felt-tip marking pen. After drawing a circle in the center of the page, he printed the words Action plan inside the circumference. Then he drew a spike from the twelve o'clock position with the words Cost reduction and use of SPC. Next, he drew a spike at two o'clock with the word Quality. "Now suppose we put down what we want to keep alive here—that's in keeping with our charter."

"Then put down corrective action," the Customer Service Manager suggested. "We have to keep that alive. We've been too successful to quit now. What we can do is use the same teams for corrective action on the TQM process."

"And add quality improvement," said the Quality Control Manager. "We want to keep going until we have a total quality system working here. I know we can do it."

The Production Manager's drawing now looked like this:

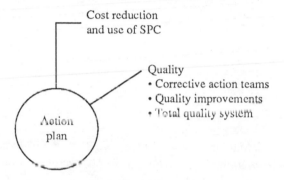

The group began to take a more avid interest as the members sensed what their activity might produce.

"Add a spike for productivity," said the Customer Service Manager. "You know what Alice says. It's no good having perfect quality if you don't pay attention to the cost of getting it. You can bankrupt the company by going further than we have to and not paying attention to productivity."

"I think I'll put down setups and throughput, too," the Production Manager said, as he added more spikes to the drawing.

"Put down JIT," the Manufacturing Services Manager requested. "And add the words pull system, stockless inventory, and zero waste."

"Don't stop there," the Accounting Manager interjected. "They want lower inventories everywhere. We have to cut them to the bone, so we can increase our working capital. Alice wants that done by the end of the year. Put inventories up there as a separate issue."

The Production Manager's diagram was expanding:

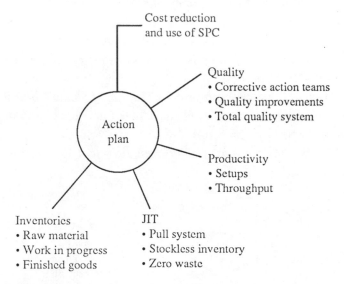

The Sales Manager, roused to the task, said, "Don't forget the management information system. That has to tie the whole thing together. Without good data and communications, everything will fall apart."

"You're right," the Accounting Manager agreed. "And put something up there about sales."

"We don't need to put that up there," the Sales Manager argued. "What does any of this have to do with sales?"

"How about the effectiveness of your sales calls?" the Production Manager asked. "Or the ability of each representative? Or the amount of sales expense per order?"

"Or the assignment of territories?" the Manufacturing Services Manager questioned.

"Those are routine matters," the Sales Manager persisted.

"When was the last time you really questioned the quality of the job being done in sales?" the Quality Control Manager asked.

"Or how much productivity your sales force is giving?" the Production Manager added.

"All right, put it down," the Sales Manager conceded.

The Manufacturing Services Manager was pointing with a pencil.

"Add a spike for recognition. If we do all this, people should get rewarded for making it happen."

The Production Manager accommodated that request and stepped back from the chart to observe the work.

"Wait a minute," the Sales Manager said with a cough. "We forgot the most important thing—our customers. Add customer satisfaction."

"If you change the name in the middle to customer satisfaction and profits," the Accounting Manager suggested, "you have the reason to do all of this."

"The whole idea is to keep customers and make money," the Sales Manager agreed. "I second the motion."

The Manufacturing Services Manager nodded his agreement. "Then you would have what they're looking for. All the issues we want to pursue. Everything they want. And more money for the effort."

"You would have what we're all here for," the Customer Service Manager corrected. "You would have all our efforts focusing on one objective."

The group smiled as they observed their emerging action plan:

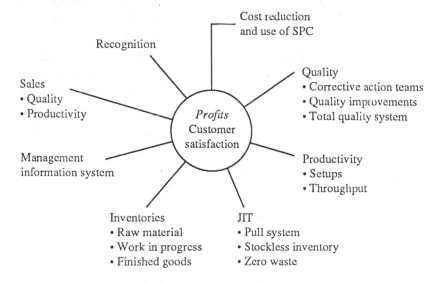

Recognition

Cost reduction
and use of SPC

Sales
• Quality
• Productivity

Quality
• Corrective action teams
• Quality improvements
• Total quality system

Profits
Customer
satisfaction

Management
information system

Productivity
• Setups
• Throughput

Inventories
• Raw material
• Work in progress
• Finished goods

JIT
• Pull system
• Stockless inventory
• Zero waste

The group discussed their work for another hour and then dispatched the Sales Manager and the Production Manager to review the plan with Alice Harper. The plan proposed the pursuit of one, all-

encompassing improvement process that featured all of the necessary ingredients for success.

"Add some targets in each area. Tell me how you will measure performance, and I'll accept the plan," was Alice's conclusion.

Alice is making a second attempt to promote significant improvement. This time she is using the team approach and has empowered her people to develop their own action plan. The plan is a road map and is a good start. But the journey will encounter many obstacles and will require that certain actions—the how of the journey—occur or there will be no progress. The individual activities to implement the process are yet to be defined. We leave Alice at this point in order to define our process for making a similar journey, before returning to check on the results of her second attempt.

Defining the Business Partnering Concept

We define business partnering as the creation of cooperative business alliances between constituencies within an organization and between an organization and its suppliers and customers. Business partnering occurs through a pooling of resources in a trusting atmosphere focused on continuous, mutual improvement. The alliances formed allow the involved parties to establish and sustain a competitive advantage over similar entities. (A few comments on what business partnering as we use the term is *not:* we are not referring to a formal legal arrangement such as a partnership nor to the pooling of resources simply to establish a larger entity.)

The features of business partnering include:

- The successful alliances formed between traditional adversaries (unions/management), quasi-combatants (buyers and sellers in a zero-sum game focused solely on attaining a price advantage), and peer groups (sales, manufacturing, accounting, and so on) to create benefits impossible to achieve through conventional methods.

- The search for and discovery of innovations, cost and productivity improvements, and quality levels that bring a new dimension to performance, reliability, and customer satisfaction. These levels are attained because members of the alliances plainly see the mutual advantages to be gained.
- The determination to sustain the relationship by fostering a process of continuous improvement that provides all parties with a long-standing competitive advantage.

In its simplest form, business partnering can be characterized *as a process of improvement that brings an organization and its constituent parts to the point where special benefits not found in competing networks can be created.* These benefits, which are mutually developed, include enhanced products or services offered, improved relationships between the involved parties, and increased consumer satisfaction. Perhaps more basically, partnering is a people thing, through which men and women from all parts of an organization—working with each other and with their suppliers and customers—commit themselves to honestly improve the relationships and performances that make a business system work and survive.

To illustrate our concept, consider the traditional relationship that exists between suppliers and customers (pictured in Figure 3.1). The two parties exist in separate worlds and negotiate for positions of greater strength on the issues of products, quantity, price, and delivery. Quality is presumed to exist. Service becomes a concern only after conclusion of the negotiations when promises are not kept.

Figure 3.2 depicts a better relationship. In the new relationship, the customer and supplier organizations have new, higher levels of capability by virtue of partnering in previously guarded turf. The purchasing department still negotiates with sales representatives, but now the production departments from both organizations have a meaningful dialogue that allows them to consider what will help both groups improve performance. Marketing allows members of the supplier's design group to sit in as new products and services are developed,

Figure 3.1. The Traditional Customer-Supplier Relationship.

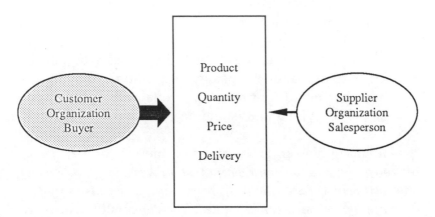

so cycle times for delivery are shortened and the innovation fits well with both group's capabilities. The partnering extends all the way to a relationship between shipping and receiving so the product is delivered not just on time but in a way that helps both firms.

The interaction between the organizations does not occur in some field of combat, but in areas of mutual interest. Within this interactive zone, resources are pooled so conversations go beyond quantity and price. Consideration is given to all the potential interactions so problems can be solved and opportunities for improvement seized. The new relationship concludes with mutual winners, not with the one winner and one loser from the traditional relationship.

Partnering must not be confused with the latest business fad, the program to be tested this month, a tool to create a momentary motivational lift, or a cosmetic attempt to avoid making necessary improvements to equipment or interpersonal conditions. Business partnering is a formula for long-term success based on the concept that people working in concert for the purpose of mutual benefit will always best people working individually for the same objective. Referring back to the continuous improvement model (Figure 2.1), we recall

Figure 3.2. An Improved Customer-Supplier Relationship.

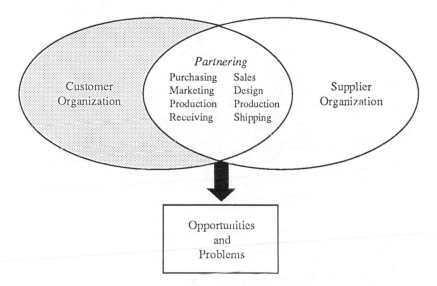

that the critique of the improvement effort highlights the need
to form alliances that do not normally exist in a business organization. Additionally, the desire to sustain the benefits of
the improvement effort into the future requires that these alliances be formalized so mutual benefits for the involved parties can accrue. These are the factors that drive business partnering. As the constituencies clearly see the advantages of
participating in a pooling of resources, they begin to willingly
give that extra effort that means the difference between success and failure in sustaining the gains. With this commitment
in place, the business organization is then prepared to make
the connection to the business partnering model.

The Business Partnering Model

The business partnering model (here illustrated for initiating
customer partnering) is described in Figure 3.3. The process
begins with a firm resolve and commitment to develop a true
partnering alliance. Next, the key people who will influence

Figure 3.3. The Business Partnering Model.

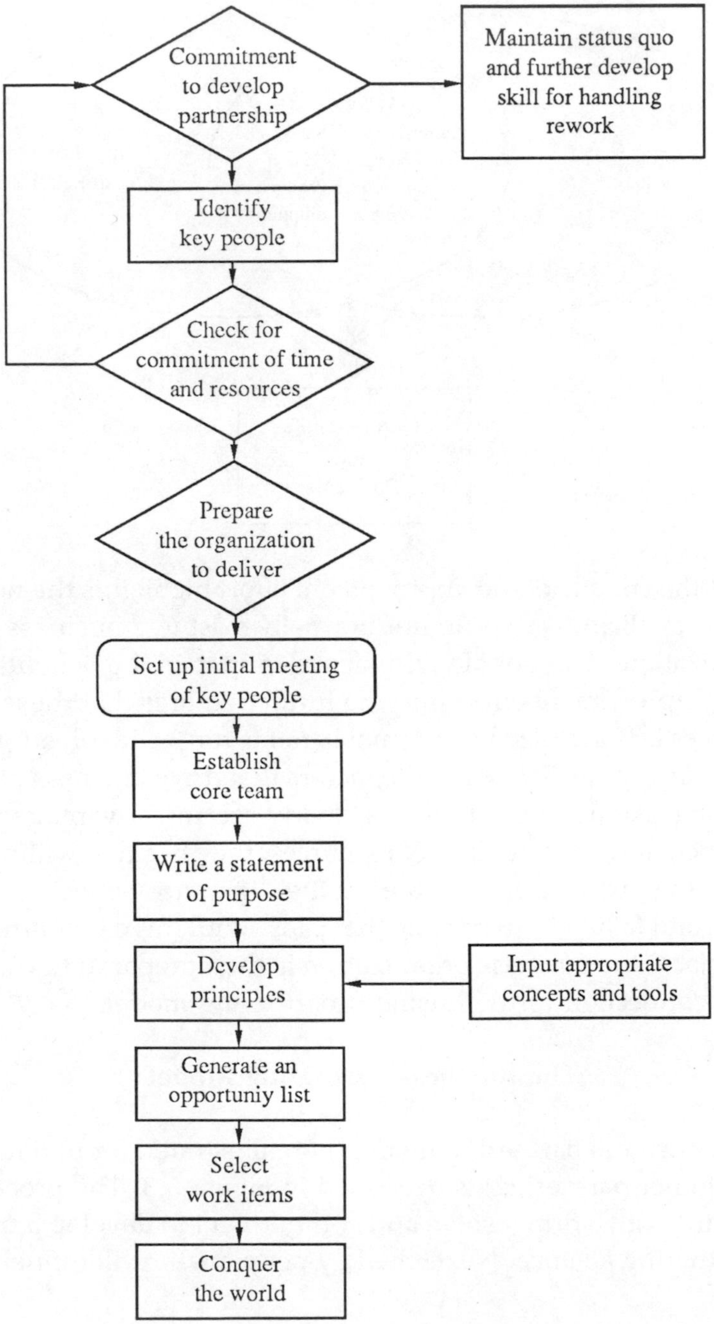

the alliance and make it happen are identified. If their commitment (beyond the philosophical buy-in) in terms of time and resources is sufficient, the process moves forward. If a full measure of determination is lacking, the model recycles. If the model recycles twice, the system should revert to the status quo, forget about partnering, and concentrate on enhancing the organization's ability to excuse poor performance.

When the proper measure of dedication is present, the parties prepare their organizations to deliver on the concept. Great reluctance can be anticipated as people bring contradictory perceptions to the discussion. Much explanation will be required to ensure proper understanding of the guiding principles. Following a meeting of the key people, a core team of implementers is established. This group takes the endorsement of the key players and produces a statement of purpose.

When this statement is approved by the key people, the core team then develops the principles that will lead to actual implementation. They do this by applying the most appropriate concepts and tools gleaned from the wealth of success stories in the improvement literature. With those principles as a guide, the team generates an opportunity list from the many issues both parties would like to resolve. In essence, the parties select their objectives and institute an improvement process. Specific actions or work items are selected from the opportunity list, and joint teams are sent to find solutions that will benefit both parties to the alliance.

The model described in Figure 3.3 has purposely been drawn in general terms, since our experience counsels that each partnering arrangement is unique. There are simply too many opportunities to pursue, too many issues to consider, and too many options on what the end results should be to force-fit the procedure into a rigid model. Flexibility has to be a feature of the relationship, but not flexible responses for the inadequacies of both parties. What is required is flexibility to meet the needs of the ultimate consumer through a mutual effort. Moving from concept to action means the parties to an alliance have taken the time and applied the resources to determine how the partnering they espouse will enhance mutual viability. When that tenet is understood, the system has a chance of succeeding.

To make this type of alliance work, it is absolutely necessary to overcome internal cultural complications. In that vein, it is appropriate to begin the illustration of our model by considering the most traditional of adversarial relationships—that between unions and management.

Beyond Collective Bargaining

After an organizational assessment increases the awareness of what is happening within an organization and the whys and hows of the business strategy are explained, employee dedication to improve generally increases. The task then becomes getting the maximum number of employees involved in the improvement process. As we have stated, a company can communicate the organization's intent and values through the effective use of mission or vision statements. The best statements clearly invite workers to become active participants in the implementation process. These statements explain:

- What the organization is chasing, that is, what are the objectives
- What will satisfy the organization's customers, internally and externally
- Where the organization will be when the improvement goals are achieved

The managerial task is now to encourage employees to help figure out how to do what has to be done.

For those organizations that have a bargaining unit as a representative of the employees, we suggest that when the normal negotiating between union and management is concluded and both sides have signed an operating agreement, the time has come to form an alliance for future viability—to go beyond collective bargaining.

The labor contract stipulates the terms under which the parties will function for a time. It does not ensure success. Labor and management have to work beyond the contract in a mutual manner to provide what customers are seeking. The typical buyer is not interested in the terms of a plant contract but is vitally concerned with the quality, delivery, and services from that plant. The elements of business partnering in the union/management relationship that would make sense to the customer include a few exercises in common sense:

- Rank-and-file members should be used as contact points with customers so the requirements of the product or service are clearly understood. Quality becomes a reality when every worker knows what the term means to the consumer. In a service organization, this means that people performing the service make direct contact with customers to discover what satisfies them. To overlook this step is to leave the definition of customer satisfaction totally in the hands of managers. The translation to the workers is invariably colored by managers' lack of contact with the final determiner of satisfaction.

- Performance and compensation have to be linked so that people within the organization share in the gain or losses that result from their effort.

- Securing the active participation of as many employees as possible in improving performance must move beyond being a conversation piece to take on permanent status. This includes pervasive employee idea generation systems, direct involvement in data gathering and statistical analysis, participation in continuous improvement actions, and some form of self-regulating teams. A world-class organization will implement five to ten usable ideas per employee per year. Some organizations now benefit from twenty to forty ideas per employee per year.

This opportunity—beyond collective bargaining—is so great that failing to tap this resource is tantamount to passing up a chance to find a hidden treasure. Armand Feigenbaum (1989, p. 69) states: "In many companies, a 'hidden organization' exists in the factory and office which results from the failure of the firm to do the job right the first time. This wastes from 15 to 40 percent of total productive capacity. There is no better way to improve productivity than to convert this hidden organization to productive use."

When managers are wise enough to secure the cooperation of the organization's bargaining unit to tap this 15–40 percent extra productivity, they have found a way to attain a wealth of improvement for a minimum of investment. Only two elements are required to gain the benefits of this potential: management must eradicate its silo thinking and must demonstrate an effective leadership orientation.

Planetree Model Hospital Project

In his book *Thriving on Chaos,* Tom Peters (1987) cites many rich examples of how to create greater customer satisfaction, a key ingredient for business success. To illustrate the application of partnering concepts, we borrow his story on the Planetree Model Hospital Project.

> Robin Orr administers the thirteen-bed Planetree Model Hospital Project at San Francisco's Pacific Presbyterian Medical Center. The typical counter between nurses and patients was the first thing to go at Planetree. The formal medical records are always open to the patient; moreover, he or she and the family are vigorously encouraged to write comments on the record. Patients are also urged to question a doctor's decision to prescribe any drug. Interaction is further facilitated by medical library privileges and the suggestion that patients should read up on

such things as their ailment, drugs, and drug side effects. The nursing arrangement provides another listening (and involvement) post. One nurse has overall responsiblity for coordinating the patient's care throughout the hospital stay and afterwards. Working with the coordinating nurse, he or she makes joint decisions about every aspect of the stay and treatment. And there's a patient advocate nurse who irons out any miscommunications between doctors, nurses, and the patient—interceding long before a minor irritant festers into a full-blown problem. Dr. Philip Lee, president of the San Francisco Health Commission (not associated with Pacific Presbyterian), says, "When patients understand the nature of their treatment, and understand how to best work with their health-care team, there is a clear evidence that shows hospital stays shorten (some studies indicated a major reduction), and returns to the hospital are far less frequent." Patients and their families rave about the program. Initially skeptical doctors are signing up in droves to take part. Orr is invited to speak about the program at meetings in cities from Dallas to Helsinki. Others are undertaking pilot projects similar to Pacific Presbyterian's. And cost per day (over and above the benefits of shorter stays and fewer repeat visits) runs no more than standard care.

Partnering can be the catalyst to make this type of sharing of improvement techniques occur. The key point is that there is too much improvement expertise—residing on separate "islands" of accomplishment—not being shared within organizations by people with similar responsiblities. Indeed, it is often easier to get help from outside resources than from those within who are capable but unwilling to help.

We offer business partnering as the sensible tool to start

an improvement process. In varying forms, it has already been done by large and small organizations, as the "best practices" have been sought within organizations. As these practices are developed and spread throughout similar business units, they invariably lead to significant improvements. Unfortunately, partnering does not occur with enough frequency nor do all of the achievers maintain their gains. Business partnering works only in the absence of silo thinking. The results are sustained when managers become leaders of the process and foster the trust and sharing necessary to keep the concepts alive.

From Concept to Action

Those organizations that have partnering efforts moving in the right direction know where they are going and what it takes to get there. The techniques they apply are simple, logical results of a dedicated and mutual effort to gain a competitive advantage:

* They begin by developing internal alliances that will ensure that commitments made to customers will be fulfilled. This means they have analyzed the areas that can create conflict between functions and units within the organization. Sales, service, and operations are linked together with a specific focus on customer satisfaction. People from all three functions, including hourly operators, have been out to see the customer, so there is no confusion regarding the definition of customer satisfaction. A dedication exists to meet and exceed customers' specifications. Accounting is very proactive, helping all functions become as prime as possible in terms of costs and productivity. Customer specifications have been translated into stretch objectives to provide the focused orientation necessary to sustain the improvement. Adversaries have put aside their traditional hostilities in favor of an organizationwide commitment to continuous improvement.

- Continuous improvement to quality—fueled by innovative input from capable members of the organization or from any of the other organizations in the total system network—is welcomed, objectively analyzed, and quickly implemented.
- Continuous improvement to the final products and services is constantly encouraged through innovation, cycle time reduction, process enhancements, appropriate sociotechnical changes, reengineering methods, and cooperative interchange in the full linkage from first input to final consumption.
- Attainment of technical superiority (in terms of systems, procedures, inventory, technology, methodology, strategy, and implementation) for the total network over competing networks is an integral part of the mission statement.
- The organization takes the concept of benchmarking seriously and constantly strives to reach the upper limits of the applicable categories.
- Suppliers are treated as genuinely important to the improvement process, not just as vendors whose prices must be constantly attacked and lowered. These suppliers are also a part of the network alliances and contribute dramatically to improvement in an atmosphere that encourages and readily accepts ideas invented outside of the organization.
- World-class communications exist in an error-free environment, with electronic linkages that are state of the art.
- Customers are linked to the network in an environment of trust, wherein information previously restricted to outside eyes is discussed and evaluated in order to improve all possible facets of the relationship.

Achieving such lofty objectives is envisioned as a three- to ten-year quest, depending on whom we interviewed. From our perspective, there is no timetable. The biggest problem is starting the process, followed by living the tenets of the effort. Our advice is to select pilot operations to prove the viability of the tenets and to progress by adding a new piece each day, much as a large jigsaw puzzle is built.

Action Study: United Services
Automobile Association (USAA)

In 1922, twenty-five army officers were so provoked by their inability to locate insurance carriers that would write policies for people in the military that they decided to establish their own carrier. This group decided to insure each other by forming a mutual association to provide the service and coverage they sought. From that simple beginning, the United Services Automobile Association (USAA) has developed into the fifth-largest insurer of privately owned automobiles and homes. In 1992, over 14,000 employees will serve more than 2.2 million members and manage more than $24 billion in assets. Member/owners of this remarkable insurance exchange remain primarily present and former military officers.

Since the time of its founding, USAA has maintained a strong commitment to providing its members with excellent products and services at a competitive price. USAA always had a very simple and straightforward business intent. Unfortunately, as is true for many organizations, growth proved a challenge to sustaining that intent. Along the way, problems of quality, productivity, and cost crept into the organization, and the commitment to excellence and competitive price was in danger. In 1968, USAA brought in a recently retired brigadier general from the Air Force, Robert F. McDermott, to strengthen the organization and to resurrect the tenets of the long-standing mission statement. The actions taken by McDermott and the reactions of the USAA organization so closely parallel the principles of business partnering that USAA provides a strong illustration of the power of mutual alliances as a catalyst to achieve necessary improvements.

When McDermott assumed command, USAA was servicing 650,000 members, but not very smoothly. In a *Harvard Business Review* interview (Teal, 1991, p. 119), he described the situation as follows: "When I arrived, I had six months to look around before I took over as CEO. And what I saw gave me second thoughts. We were good on claims, we were good on price, we were honest and honorable. In most other categories, we fell short. . . . There were a lot of small departments . . . mostly run by warlords who didn't communicate with one another. They fought perpetual turf battles. Actuarial didn't speak to underwriting, and claims didn't speak to either one. No horizontal communication. No one knew how the whole thing fitted together, they just knew and cared about their own little piece of the company."

Plainly, USAA was suffering from the type of silo thinking that greatly inhibits attaining higher performance. And what of the singular focus on excellent service? There was ample evidence that attention to the mission statement had not been reinforced by an oriented leadership. McDermott elaborated on one particular example of leadership acceptance of poor performance. "There was paper everywhere. You can't imagine how much paper . . . and of course a lot of it got lost. On any given day the chances were 50–50 that we'd be able to put our hands on any particular file. In fact, so much of it got lost that, depending on the season, we had from 20 to 30 young people from local colleges who worked at night finding files."

McDermott went back to the basics that he felt characterized USAA. His intention was to develop a culture and an attitude that continuous improvement be attained in the performance of every employee. He determined to accomplish this by emphasizing employee practices and the provision of superior service to customers.

Four basic criteria were established:

- Technology would become a major vehicle to improve operations, particularly in the automation of USAA's policy-writing system. The objective was to bring state-of-the-art processing into the system so all employees would increase their capabilities to service customers.
- The organization would be properly sized for its scale of operations. Initially, that meant there would be a headcount reduction. But true to the people orientation McDermott wanted to foster, displacements were to occur through attrition.

- Education and training were to be key features of the improvement process, as USAA created its own internal university to enhance employee skills, focusing on quality, prompt response, accuracy, and customer satisfaction.
- The organizational structure would be decentralized so decisions affecting policyholders (all members of USAA) would be made as close as possible to the point of contact.

These criteria accomplished significant improvements throughout USAA. The combination of user-friendly technological features and empowerment of employees to make decisions affecting customer service worked wonders. An important innovation was the introduction of image processing. Information on any particular customer, including any recent correspondence, was immediately accessed and imaged on a computer screen in front of the service representative. Since the representative also had the authority to make changes to the policy or to authorize certain payments, the customer received a positive feeling of personal service not common in the insurance business.

By appealing to employee pride, McDermott further enhanced performance and strengthened the leadership/employee alliance he wanted to foster. He established an orientation that encouraged people to grow to their maximum potential. As part of this process, USAA moved to a four-day work week and greatly expanded its educational format. In 1991, the commitment for training and education was $19 million (2.7 percent of the annual budget). USAA also employs over 200 full-time instructors to implement the strong commitment to improving employee capabilities. Concurrently, actions were taken to ensure equitable hiring and promotional policies, and employees were cross-trained to enrich their work life and prepare them to fill key positions.

We view these actions as consistent with the principles of partnering. USAA extended those principles to customer relationships with equally important positive results. Part of USAA's original mission statement was that the organization would provide special benefits to its customers. In support of this policy, USAA had no war clause that most insurance carriers apply to prevent payouts in the event a customer is killed in armed conflict. During the Desert Storm action in the Middle

East, USAA maintained coverage and sold new policies to members called into action. This decision further solidified USAA's alliance with its members. For this organization, customer service is ranked ahead of profit and growth as key drivers.

In a similar vein, McDermott also instituted a practice of analyzing and deciding what services the member/customers wanted from USAA. With data gathered from USAA's extensive customer base, McDermott discovered that members wanted a wider array of services in addition to basic insurance coverage. In response, USAA added a comprehensive line of personal financial services. McDermott explains this action: "We are not just an insurance company anymore. Our success has been brought on by diversification and expansion into products and services which meet our members' changing needs" (Ginnodo, 1991, p. 2).

Growth is now well managed at USAA, with excellent results in terms of service. The current organization handles more than 110 million pieces of incoming and outgoing mail annually. Employees ensure that the 100,000 telephone calls that arrive daily are handled with the best possible service. So good is the quality of that handling that the Quality and Productivity Management Association (QPMA) made USAA the recipient of its 1991 Leadership Award. As part of the documentation for presenting this honor, these comments were made: "USAA's management and employees see outstanding services as a cultural imperative that also makes good business sense. The Association's people strive for reliability and predictability in dealing with members and customers. They seek to build long-term relationships with members and their families by providing quality products and services that meet their changing needs. . . . Selection as a finalist in both the 1989 and 1990 Malcolm Baldrige National Quality Award program testified to USAA's commitment to total quality. . . . That commitment extends to maintaining a professional and motivated workforce whose daily job performance reflects the quality values and ideals of the Association and its members" (Ginnodo, 1991, p. 3).

McDermott summarized the orientation that has succeeded for USAA in answer to this *Harvard Business Review* interview question: Isn't there ever a conflict between altruism and profit? McDermott characterized the internal culture in terms that show partnering and profits are natural allies, rather than conflicting principles: "What you call core competence and strategy and altruism and mission are all the same thing for USAA. They're all a matter of community. This company has formed a bond with its members. We're a family" (Teal, 1991, p. 127).

Summary

Our experiences have dramatically demonstrated that business partnering—the building of alliances for mutual benefit throughout an organization's business network—can have a major, positive impact on the results of a continuous improvement effort. The power of partnering comes from its capacity to unite various constituencies and their leaders in support of common objectives, with mutual benefits for the effort.

The alliances that form the central part of the partnering process must supercede normal business arrangements: they need to go beyond the terms of a collective bargaining agreement or traditional interdepartmental relationships. The alliances necessary to make partnering a success have to extend to all constituencies affecting the organization and must bind them to a mutually beneficial improvement effort.

Chapter Four

◆

THE ROLE
OF MANAGEMENT

In this chapter, we detail the crucial role that managers and leaders must play if the partnering process is to succeed. Managers can ensure that partnering is done properly or allow the many cultural inhibitors that exist in most organizations to defeat the process. The secret, of course, is management's steadfast support and reinforcement of both the principles that make partnering a sensible catalyst in the improvement process and of the formation of the necessary alliances.

Before describing how these requirements should be accomplished, we return to Alice Harper and observe a series of performance reviews that shows progress comes only when the entire organization accepts the improvement tenets, senses benefit for those who make the necessary effort, and moves forward as a united force. Our purpose is to illustrate how failure occurs because parts of an organization go forward, while other parts are offsetting the gains and moving in the reverse direction. It is this latter reality that Alice must grasp before she can succeed in her endeavor.

Alice Goes One Forward, Two Back

It had taken another eighteen months for the empowered participants to attempt the implementation of a Total Quality Management (TQM) system. After that time, progress in Alice Harper's unit was rated as flat. "At least we stabilized the situation," was the best she could conclude.

During that year, Alice had made some changes. She had hired a senior buyer and replaced the production and accounting managers with recruits provided by a placement agency. These moves were made primarily because Alice concluded that changes would stimulate a move in the right direction. There had been some notable enhancements, such as the shop floor reporting system, the hot line for customer complaints, and the new waste reduction program. Unfortunately, the end results did not reflect real improvement over former levels of performance.

The shop floor data was now rid of false entries and clearly pin-pointed the poor performance operations. Concentration on those areas, however, had not increased total throughput, so much of the volume increase that was generated by the "customer-focused" sales effort could not be filled. Back orders had increased, and the new hot line was flooded by customers trying to expedite orders. The waste reduction program had increased material yields, but units per hour had declined.

Alice determined that she would use her performance reviews, an exercise she faithfully executed, as a vehicle to try and find some answers.

The first of these reviews was with the Sales Manager. The discussion went routinely until the subject of sales revenues was reached.

"The fact is," Alice began, "our revenues are flat for the third year in a row. That's not progress, especially in a market that has been up 3 percent a year."

The Sales Manager squirmed in her chair.

"There is no way you can criticize me here, Alice," she retorted. "If manufacturing could have made the product, we could have sold it. Our demand is up. We simply haven't filled the orders."

"How about price?" Alice parried. "You are down 5 percent in selling price."

"We had to do that, Alice. Your quality expert has made everyone aware of quality, including the customers. We used to be able to get them to take whatever we made. Now they want to send it back or get credits."

"Aren't you happy that we are trying to make the product right?"

"Sure I am, but now the customers know the difference. That 5 percent amounts to discounts for poor performance. You have to shape

up the production group, Alice. Start making good product and deliver it on time, and I'll get that 5 percent, and more, back."

"We need the price, and the volume, now," Alice persisted. "Your job is to figure out how we do that. I'll put pressure on manufacturing, but it takes time."

The Sales Manager shrugged indifferently. "Look, Alice, we all agreed to the game plan. I put my name on it. But it isn't happening. Remember JIT? We were supposed to ship just in time. Our on-time deliveries were being reported at 95 percent. You put in an accurate system, and it turns out to be 80 percent. Now I have people screaming that we stink. We don't have the luxury of time. We're farming out orders now. If something doesn't get better soon, volume and price will slip some more."

A later review with the Production Manager contained a different conversational segment. After discussing the volume decline and the poor customer ratings, he made this comment, "Alice, we are making progress. We're rolling the plate much faster than we used to, and the quality is much better."

"I know," Alice agreed. "But we don't get any more product out the door. Are you concentrating on the right things to improve?"

The Production Manager sighed audibly. "Let's start at the top, Alice. We've been telling people to do it right. I don't think we even agree on it!"

"What do you mean?"

"To me, 'it' means getting only good product, totally within specifications, to the customer. I'm gearing my people, my machines, and my suppliers to give me just that."

"Where's the problem then?" Alice asked.

"We have a sales department that says our it is out of date. They say the customers want something new, something fresher, whatever that means. We also have sales reps coming to me saying give me more of the it we're making regardless of quality. They say they have orders to fill and they don't want their customers to find other suppliers while we fix our system."

"Look," Alice said. "We are going to have quality. Your job is to find the means to do that. If we need innovation or new products, we'll handle that through marketing. I want you concentrating on more throughput, with every unit meeting specifications."

"But what if those specs are wrong?"

"What do you mean?"

"How long has it been since we challenged these specifications? We can do things to make more product, but that sales department of yours could get the customer to help us, if they wanted. I know we have some customers that can use looser tolerances. That would save me . . . "

Alice interrupted, "I want the same quality standards for all customers. I want every unit to be completely within spec."

"Then you will have to accept lower speeds," he replied.

The review with the Accounting Manager was the least confrontational. Alice had expressed general satisfaction with results in the financial area. She was particularly complimentary when discussing the new shop floor reports.

"At least I have data that is reliable," she commented.

"Reliable, but not where it should be," was the Accounting Manager's reply. "I'm trying to give manufacturing activity-based information and do it in a proactive way, but I feel there should be more response."

"What are you looking for?"

"Well, we know now what each product really costs. If we functioned as a team around here, we should use that information to sell to our strengths. That's the way to maximize profits."

"What if the customer wants the things we have high costs on or wants the full lines?" Alice shot back.

"Then we have to fill the orders and get better at what we do," she replied. "In the meantime, we have to survive. Can we get sales to help manufacturing by selling to the things we do best?"

"That's running away from the issue," Alice protested. "We all agreed on a plan to get total quality, everywhere throughout the company. Sure I can tell sales to push certain products, but I want to run an organization that can make whatever the market wants, and make it well."

"I don't know if we can do that, Alice. It seems to me more companies are focusing on what they do best."

The Quality Control Manager accepted the appraisal with thanks and promised to work hard to improve in the designated areas. Before leaving Alice's office, she asked, "Are you going to stick with our improvement plan?"

"That's my intention," Alice responded. "Why do you ask?"

"Well, it's just that we put so much work into it, and I know you're disappointed in the results."

"You've got that right," Alice sighed.

"And you have a right to be upset and to make changes. I just feel we have a good road map. We just aren't following it. We're getting sidetracked too much. If we just stay with it, I'm sure we'll have something good to show for the effort."

"I wish I could share your enthusiasm," Alice said. "But I don't have much more time. The people I report to are being very patient with me. I have to show something good—soon—or you might have a new boss."

"The logic behind the plan is solid, Alice. We worked it out for ourselves. If it doesn't work, we only have ourselves to blame. What we need is more acceptance, more dedication."

"Everyone on my staff told me they accepted the plan. They all gave me their endorsement." As she reflected on the previous reviews, Alice began to wonder. "Perhaps there wasn't as much conviction as I thought. Maybe we don't have dedication in all parts of the group."

"We need to be more of a team, Alice," was the Quality Control Manager's conclusion. "We worked out the plan together, but now it seems like it's somebody else's plan. I don't see the ownership we first showed. I know I was very excited when we drew up that plan for you. I thought sure we had it this time."

"Problem is," Alice sighed, "we go one step forward, and then take one step backward."

"No!" came the correction. "We go one forward and two back. Every time we cancel out a gain with a loss, we lose someone from the effort. We started with a very enthused group. We keep losing some of that enthusiasm each day."

Alice remains in the midst of her dilemma. Something is eluding her. She has tried to orient her leadership. Her managers tried to set aside their silo thinking in favor of a jointly developed, multifaceted plan. Yet the positive results simply have not developed. One thing we know with certainty is that the strength of the plan is not enough to ensure success. Alice has an improvement initiative, but she needs help in getting it working. She cannot replace everyone. She has to find something that will generate the correct actions for her specific environment and inspire her people to willingly and correctly implement the process.

We have generated an improvement model and a set of world-class standards as a goal. These elements help, but they do not guarantee success. The next step is to fit the features of the model to the circumstances of the situation. One of the most effective ways to accomplish that task is to have managers assume a leadership role and guide the process to its logical conclusion.

Effective Leadership Orientation

An entire book could be written on the correct leadership approach to bring success to a partnering effort and enhance continuous improvement. For our purposes here, we focus on five factors that we have found to be present when success is achieved and sustained. These factors are imperatives that must be observed if the type of alliances we suggest are to develop and endure.

•   *Effective leaders make certain the organization is prepared for the change process.* Key managers and representatives of the key constituencies must be brought together to discuss both the level of acceptance of the improvement logic and the readiness to implement. Leaders need to know clearly whether or not the group is prepared to execute. Direct confrontation, third-party facilitation, professional counseling, or some combination of techniques can be utilized. There can be no hidden inhibitions or the improvement process will stall and fail. The wise leader moves forward only when the constituencies can be counted on to apply the improvement logic. When such a state of readiness is not present, the leader should work on understanding and commitment rather than forcing the effort forward.

• *Effective leaders articulate the overall mission, vision, or task that must be accomplished in simple, acceptable terms.* If the improvement effort is to succeed, the implementers need a concept, a statement, or a simple list of ideas that make enough sense to rally their total effort. So long as they withhold energy because they do not accept the logic being foisted on them, the system will suboptimize. Chances of success increase as the leaders present a message so powerful that all those latent energies are freely expended. Our experiences have consistently shown that the best success stories come from organizations where the guiding mission or vision statement was simple and sound and was delivered by leaders in such a convincing manner that people within the organization, selected at random, could clearly repeat the driving message—with enthusiasm.

• *Effective leaders work with the constituencies to develop the desired end results and mutual benefits.* To legislate the matrix of improvement necessities from the top of the organization is a mistake. Short-term fixes are all that can result. Successful improvement of a lasting nature derives when the matrix is developed with top-down, bottom-up, and side-to-side input. In this manner, all constituencies feel ownership and exhibit cooperative behavior because the matrix has mutual meaning. Formation of the internal alliances we consider so important starts when the groups can step back, look at the improvement targets, and see the mutual benefits because they see their authorship.

• *Effective leaders model the behavior that the improvement process demands of all constituents.* Continuous improvement and business partnering do not occur if leaders decree such actions will happen and then do not apply the requisite disciplines to themselves. Leaders in search of excellent performance have to be excellent role models. They have to develop practices that reinforce the improvement logic and then get out among the constituent groups and demonstrate those practices. Business partnering demands that leaders be active participants whose every action supports the driving logic of the effort.

• *Effective leaders provide the necessary resources.* Business partnering means that leaders and followers function as though their mutual efforts are essential to organizational success. It also means they are working together, so all can draw satisfaction from the results of their efforts. Along the way, members of various constituencies will indicate that further progress is possible if certain resources are available. If leaders consistently deny the provision of these resources, a feeling of being cheated will quickly arise. If new capital funds are short, then that condition should be explained early and acceptable budgets introduced. As other noncapital resources—such as executive attention, employee time, specialist talent, temporary work groups, and so forth—are requested, the wise leader supplies them. Good faith is the usual result, and the chances of success are enhanced.

With the proper executive orientation and the eradication of silo thinking, the organization has immeasurably increased its potential for success. Partnering becomes a reality under these conditions because the constituencies see mutual benefit, good role models, and a sensible direction that inspires their full support.

Value of Constancy

The primary responsibility of management is to precisely determine the direction the enterprise must follow to be successful—and then to be consistent in following that course. This does not negate the obvious need to be flexible in the face of the rapidly changing conditions that characterize today's business environment. It means managers should adjust for changes in situation but should remain faithful to the direction and supporting ideas that have motivated performance. An analogy could be to a sea captain, who must adjust course or tactics during a violent storm. The business captain must similarly make adjustments under demanding circumstances. Managers must fully explain the need for adjustment (not alteration), keep changes to a necessary minimum, and return to course quickly. The alternative is to "jerk" the organization about in troubled waters, greatly increasing the risk of confusion and drops in performance. We call such a practice *management by jerks* (MBJ).

We do not employ this terminology to suggest that *managers* are jerks; rather, we aver that many business organizations suffer from managers whose *actions* tend to jerk their people about unmercifully. Such managers spring too quickly after the latest leadership vogue instead of providing a clear and constant vision. The antithesis of clear, motivational leadership is, unfortunately, a muddled continuum of jerks in various directions, often for conflicting purposes. This style of management leaves the organization in a state of constant confusion and suboptimization.

W. Edwards Deming's first (of fourteen) points for management is "Create constancy of purpose." The Japanese, who credit Deming for the philosophy that drove their spectacular growth and success, apparently learned this lesson well. Their single purpose—to attain world domination of markets through quality, people, technology, and innovation—needs little endorsement. The results offer adequate substantiation of the Deming creed.

A counterargument could be presented that it is necessary to try new techniques and to introduce new paradigms if managers are to guide employees to greater achievements. We heartily agree! To accomplish objectives never before achieved, an organization has to try techniques never before utilized, but such an approach does not have to be in conflict with constancy of purpose. It is only necessary that the new techniques result in accomplishment of the goals that are required for success in the current business environment.

Characteristics of MBJ

Management by jerks (MBJ) is characterized by a confusing series of strategy changes, which are labeled by the sponsoring managers as crucial for current conditions but interpreted by progressively more frustrated and cynical employees as the "flavor of the month." Through their frustration—and especially because of their cynicism—these employees create a chain reaction of nonperformance that leads to organizational paralysis. This paralysis results in the enterprise becoming lethargic, ineffective, and resistant to making the continuous improvement so necessary for today's competitive survival.

The improvements engendered under MBJ tend to develop with difficulty and result in "accomplishments by jerks"—short-term, isolated gains that fail to result in lasting achievement. The organization that suffers from MBJ is constantly regaining the same ground. That means the employees endlessly pursue the same objectives but in differing manners, because they do not hold the gains under one or more of their previous jerks in strategy. Waste will decline—only to rise again. Inventories will be reduced—only to come back in larger magnitudes. Market shares go up—and fall back. Costs ebb and flow as the various inconstant purposes are pursued and canceled—to be replaced by the latest technique touted in the business press.

Of Visions and Missions

Why MBJ leads to lack of improvement, sluggish performance, cynical frustration, operational paralysis, and inhibiting fear is easy to comprehend. Most employees know what to do.

Confusion arises when they don't know why they are doing it or how to balance the competing priorities. It is incumbent upon oriented managers to help workers understand the importance of their actions and then allow them to express themselves as they perform. In the process, people want to be recognized for their accomplishments. Put simply, they want to do something meaningful, please the boss in the process, and be rewarded and recognized for the effort. If the boss has presented a clear and constant vision that has mutual meaning, the employees know what is needed and will work to satisfy— and also to anticipate—the requirements of the vision.

On the other hand, if the boss presents a confused, unclear, or fluctuating vision of the company's direction, employees will be unsure what has to be accomplished or why. There will be real fear of making the wrong decision. Indeed, the correct decision for yesterday may be viewed as improper for today's jerk. Consequently, employees will not be able to anticipate the needs as expressed by management, and that condition will paralyze operations. Employees will wait interminably for direction "from the top," resulting in a firm that is slow in responding to customers and that experiences decreasing self-esteem.

Mission statements can be powerful tools in mitigating these symptoms of MBJ. Unfortunately, they tend to be exercises in short-term energy, with an emphasis on quick publication and virtually no follow-through on the intentions prescribed by the statement. They don't have to be like this. Because well-conceived, thoughtful mission statements are so valuable (both in articulating management policies and encouraging employee support of the organization's direction), the next section considers how to use them to motivate an organization.

Using Mission Statements as Motivators

Entire volumes have been written on how to develop mission/value/purpose statements that will inspire an organization and improve total performance. In the interest of brevity, we leave those volumes to the reader's reference and consider here the elements of such statements that will have positive impact for an organization pursuing the concept of business partnering.

The stages through which an organization should progress to successfully motivate its constituents (using statements) are as follows:

•   *Develop the organizational intent at the senior level.* Time should be allotted with this busiest of groups to reach consensus on where the organization is and where it must go. Poor execution at this point will lead directly to mixed signals and cosmetic endorsement. The output of this stage is a tacit explanation of the purpose for which the organization exists. This intention must reflect current conditions and also be suitable for tomorrow's environment. In essence, it should reflect the attitude of the leadership group regarding "why we are here."

•   *Transcribe the organizational intent into a statement that is concise, understandable, inspirational, easily articulated, and powerful enough to mobilize effort at all levels.* We prefer a succinct, personal vision statement followed by the specific mission. A vision statement should clearly communicate the superordinate accomplishment(s) the organization wants to achieve. It should be inspirational, not maudlin. It should be brief, not exceeding one paragraph. It should incite enthusiasm, but not fears that sights have been set too high. The best visions include an accomplishment that has never before been achieved (for example, NASA's vision to be the first to land people on the moon). Employees should read the vision statement and develop the feeling that execution will make them special—not necessarily elite, but somehow above the crowd.

A mission statement communicates what the members of the organization will do, as a team, to enact the vision. Each unit of the organization has to be able to interpret the mission statement and know what it has to do. The statement needs to be operationally specific at the macrolevel and to span line and support responsibilities.

• *Establish the strategic priorities for the near and long term.* Those who read the vision/mission statement of the organization should be inspired to want to make it happen, and they will quickly begin questioning what the priorities should be and how potential conflicts should be handled. That means they need a focus for their efforts. The third step in the process assimilates input from the practical implementers and the visionaries to establish a coherent set of priorities. These are statements that identify how resources will be allocated to accomplish major goals.

• *Set the strategic goals and objectives.* The tendency of most organizations is to jump to this step without establishing priorities. That is a mistake! In the fourth step, the organization gets specific, with priorities firmly in hand. Now the requirements to meet the demands of the vision/mission statements are defined. Accountability for successful implementation also starts at this point.

• *Delineate the key supporting principles and values.* A refinement occurs in the fifth step as the organization fits culture with action plans. How the units will promote organization-wide teamwork is defined. The values that everyone must support are presented. Again, the emphasis is on inspiration without being corny.

• *Develop the leadership qualities and traits that will ensure successful implementation.* The worst assumption an organization can make is that the managerial group is fully prepared to enact the typically lofty intentions of the vision/mission statements. Successful implementation requires an enormous amount of understanding and perseverance, particularly when cultural alterations have to be accomplished. Should empowerment to lower levels and upward policy deployment become designed features, relearning of leadership characteristics will be mandatory. Much has been written about the need to switch from managerial skills to leadership skills. This sixth step is included for such rethinking and retraining.

• *Establish a feedback loop to return necessary insights from all stakeholders.* The second worst mistake an organization can make is assuming that the vision/mission is so powerful that successful implementation is a certainty. There must be feedback—via verbal and written communication, surveys, opinions, and so forth. This feedback deserves attention and response and should find its way into modification of the priorities, values, strategies, and tactics. The vision/mission remains inspirational as it is honestly tested against results and reactions.

The Institute, a Houston-based organization that has spent considerable time helping organizations define and build direction statements, likens the exercise to that of building a bridge. We strongly endorse this approach. Figure 4.1 is its depiction of how the direction statement spans the gap from where an organization presently is and where it is going. From this "current state" to the "future state," the necessary pillars are placed to support the bridge that will move the organization to where it has to be. The bridge—and its ability to carry the organization into the future—is only as good as the effort that goes into the construction of the supporting members. The bridge will either succeed for decades or quickly collapse in today's business environment depending on the strength of that underpinning.

The additional support we would add to this depiction is a pillar labeled *consistency*. The whole bridge tumbles if the pillars are variable and constantly changing. Leaders at all levels have to maintain that constancy we have discussed to

Figure 4.1. The Direction Statement Bridge.

Source: The Institute, Inc. Used by permission.

reassure the members of the organization that the pillars have both strength and permanence. Successful reassurance may be more difficult than anticipated because most organizations have been guilty of MBJ at some time in their history.

Avoiding MBJ

The reality of business is that the central message of an organization—embodying its intent, direction, objectives, and values—must be clearly articulated, readily understood, and constantly reinforced. In the absence of clarity, individuals at any point in the enterprise will formulate their own interpretation, and the jerks will be set in motion. How, then, does an organization understand this reality and avoid MBJ?

Beginning at the top, senior officials will have their discussions and disputes—hopefully to ensure the strength and validity of their arguments. When the discussions and confrontations are over, it is crucial that these officers go forth as a united group, with one voice, espousing one mission. This is constancy of purpose.

At the middle level of the organization, the mission must not be diluted. As the mission is promulgated, the temptation will loom to utilize the latest scheme or technique appearing in the business journals. If such a concept improves the central course of action, the employees will not be confused. If everyone works every day at properly communicating the ship's direction, the crew will reach the destination in the quickest and safest time. If the crew receives instead a stream of jerks, the ship will bounce from iceberg to iceberg and limp into port long after its competition. Should an employee, at any level, discover a new paradigm, idea, or technique that will shorten the trip or cut the expense, necessary adjustments should be quickly discussed, communicated, and absorbed. The voyage actually becomes more pleasurable that way. Continuing our analogy, the crew understands why the changes were made and moves to a new level of performance because the trip is now better for everyone.

When a business manager decides a midcourse correction is necessary, a simple safeguard can help avoid an MBJ reaction. The new idea should be tested against the current course using the following two questions:

- *How will the message be received?* An answer can be found by querying a few reliable confidants, who understand well the organizational culture.
- *Will the action make an adjustment to course or result in an alternative course?* The potential consequences of the action should be examined and a value (positive or negative) placed on each outcome.

The manager must explain the new course to the organization and should keep in mind that people have become disposed to expect MBJ. So even in the face of logic or necessity, employees will assume a change is a jerk. The manager must explain any change in action extremely well or expect the typical delay in implementation.

Action Study: Leaf, Inc.

Among those business organizations in our network, the one that most clearly demonstrates the positive characteristics considered in this chapter is Leaf, Inc. Leaf is a $600 million producer of confectionary items that include such well-known candies as Heath Bar, Jolly Rancher, Good & Plenty, and Milk Duds. This organization decided in the mid 1980s to embark on an improvement effort that was eventually termed Operations Improvement Program (OIP). The initial purposes were to:

- Mobilize the corporate commitment to excellence and improvement
- Develop a shared vision that would ensure full employee support
- Create a focus on problem solving as the key improvement tool

Convinced that operational improvements were essential to gain a competitive advantage, Leaf managers framed the original objectives around four key factors:

- Reduction in cycle time, so inventories would be reduced to the absolute minimum (thereby ensuring the freshness of the product)
- Improving quality to industry-leading standards
- Improving the quality of work life for all members of the firm
- Improving profitability of the business

To attain these goals, Leaf embarked on an assessment that would benchmark it against its nine largest competitors. This assessment was initially very sobering, as the benchmark grid revealed the following:

Leaf	*Competition*
Many factories	Few factories
Old factories	New factories
Poor yields (throughput)	Efficient yields
High overhead	Low overhead
Many products	Few products
	+10–15 percent margins

By focusing on the best companies in the business, Leaf was able to accurately assess its market position, concluding that major change was required for it to remain competitive, let alone attain an advantage. Leaf's studies clearly showed that strengthening its position would require a broad-based improvement effort with full support from all constituencies, including suppliers. After much analysis and very sober reasoning, management determined to embark on an across-the-board change process that would result in the following improvements:

- Creation of market-focused plants
- Enhanced international presence
- New performance measures
- Greater decentralization
- World-class, user-friendly information systems

- Enhanced reputation with customers
- Broad planning strategy
- Emphasis on positive cultural aspects
- Greater capacity utilization
- Greater vertical integration with shared objectives

In brief, Leaf decided that to compete effectively in the 1990s, a new business strategy was needed. That necessity translated into building a marketing, sales, manufacturing, and financial plan that would leapfrog Leaf ahead of its benchmarks. Manufacturing was to concentrate on facilities that were market focused, efficient, flexible, and very cost effective on limited product lines. That charter mandated consolidation, modernization, and simplification of its highly variable batch processing to a continuous operation with very narrow variation. Functional improvement programs were to be introduced in the areas of maintenance, quality, materials management, supply management, service logistics, and information technology support.

A special feature that helped this major undertaking was the use of Simultaneous Engineering (SE). As an example, when Leaf decided to consolidate all chewing gum and baseball cards into one operation, SE was used to begin transformation of the physical plant concurrent with development of the marketing and sales plan and the engineering of new capabilities. The result was a factory with the best cutting and printing tolerances in that market.

As the manufacturing process was being pursued, an organizational strategy was devised. This strategy focused on organizational development of the people, positions, and functional operations that would increase the chances of success. Selection of specific skills became the recruiting norm, and education was provided throughout the organization to enhance those skills. Much attention was directed to communications so the teams working on the improvements would understand clearly their role and mission. In this way, Leaf literally attempted to build the culture it wanted—and knew it needed to succeed.

The combination of functional improvement programs and a supporting organizational strategy led Leaf to the realization that three ingredients were essential to success:

- A continuous, visible leadership commitment, supported by in-volved actions
- Real acceptance of the change concepts and support from *all* em-ployees
- A set of common goals, clearly described in understandable lan-guage

With these ingredients, managers were convinced that Leaf could become what the senior management group described as a "fully in-tegrated manufacturer with a focus on better services to the customer."

By placing heavy emphasis on employee involvement, manage-ment sought to act out their belief in the value of the "vertical integra-tion with shared values" plank in their improvement platform. A dual effort of deploying the OIP objectives and necessities downward while sincerely seeking deployed suggestions upward was initiated. This part of the process began slowly, as managers focused attention on yields, on-time deliveries, higher inventory turns, lower delay times, better qual-ity, and greater utilization of capacity.

As Jim Grubiak, senior vice president of operations, reported, man-agers were initially disappointed because, in spite of their enthused en-dorsement of the change process, they received few written suggestions (personal communication, 1991). Determination prevailed, however, as they embarked on awareness sessions in which members of the man-agement team modified their traditional leadership roles and went directly to the factories. There they conducted what we would term a search for the heart of nonimplementation. They held a series of five-to-ten–minute interviews with employees, covering workplace condi-tions, the changing company policies, the need for training, and manage-ment's sincere interest in obtaining employee input. This effort forced the key managers to learn how to honestly interact with the people most critical to executing the principles of the OIP process. It also made man-agers realize where they had failed to change their preferred method of operation for the good of the improvement process.

The results of these sessions validated the worth of direct leader-ship involvement and a willingness to change behavior to benefit the effort. By focusing on making the company better, managers and workers began to see competition as their joint enemy. Suggestions jumped from a negligible level to three per employee. These suggestions were prioritized, approved, and implemented with quick, positive feedback being given to employees. Eight weeks after this phase of OIP was launched, the priority list showed 50 percent top-down and 50 percent bottom-up as the originators of the improvement selection criteria.

A steering committee was selected of five to seven individuals, representing both management and hourly employees. This group focused on forming teams to address the prioritized list, allocating necessary resources, monitoring team progress, and structuring the team problem-solving training they knew would be necessary. Eventually, action teams were formed, with three to seven members, focused on the top priority projects. These problem-solving teams spent two to six hours per week searching for alternative solutions and making recommendations to management. The results were a significant increase in employee involvement and reported satisfaction, lower operating costs, and a better quality of work life. The first year's savings were reported to be $6 million (from over a thousand projects).

Jim Grubiak truly believes those enhanced earnings are incidental to the quality of working life and employee satisfaction ratings. The enhanced safety performance particularly elates him. In the next phase of OIP, it is his intention to continue that focus on employees as five new initiatives are added to the improvement effort:

- Encouraging management commitment to leadership skills
- Creating the best possible organizational climate for all employees
- Driving fear out of all parts of the organization
- Formalizing the recognition system
- Enhancing the communication/problem-solving features of the process

One example does not illustrate an entire corporate effort, but the results of the Cicero, Illinois, plant tell a tale of dedication that worked, under skilled leadership.

	Before	*After*
Grievances	1/day	1/two months
Sanitation	Pass/Fail	Excellent
Attendance disciplines	3/week	1/two months
Drug/alcohol disciplines	1/week	1/two months
Efficiency	80 percent	90 percent
Safety (loss-time accidents)	251/year	40/year
Compliance to schedule	60 percent	85 percent

Summary

In this chapter, we have examined the critical role of management in ensuring the success of continuous improvement efforts and business partnering. Managers must determine the direction of the organization and then be consistent in following that course; they must exhibit what Deming calls "the constancy of purpose." Management by jerks (MBJ)—a confusing series of strategy changes—produces organizational paralysis and suboptimal organizational performance.

Organizations not paralyzed by MBJ achieve consistent records of accomplishment. Consider the constancy of purpose, mission, vision, and performance of the following:

- Motorola, with its drive for quality
- 3M, with its dedication to continual innovation
- McDonald's, with its focus on quality, service, and cleanliness
- IBM and Federal Express, with their focus on customer service
- Westinghouse, with its emphasis on reducing cycle time

Managers must motivate their organizations to achieve such performance, and there is simply no substitute for an inspired statement of purpose and the supporting visions to accomplish that task. Managers can take the time and care to issue carefully worded mission/vision statements, or they can simply be consistent in words and actions as they lead employees to continuous improvement and a competitive advantage.

Chapter Five

◆

How To
Get Started

We have previously discussed (in Chapter Two and Chapter Four) the requirements of Phase 1 (cultural analysis) of the continuous improvement model: an assessment and understanding of how the improvement process will function within an organization's existing cultural framework and the articulation of organizational objectives and strategies. In this chapter, we move on to elaborate the analysis process of Phase 2 (development of action plan) that translates the objectives and strategies of management into an operating strategy. We begin in the logical first place — within the organization itself. We believe that the internal house should be put in order before proceeding externally. Since getting started requires dealing with obstacles to successful execution of the change process, we return to Alice Harper and her group for a reminder of what types of action impede an improvement effort.

Alice at the Crossroads

Bothered by her unit's flat results, Alice called a meeting of her direct reports to consider why they had not made more progress.

"It should be obvious," she began, looking at no one in particular, "that we are going nowhere fast with TQM [Total Quality Management]. After a full year, I see no positive results. On the basis of our progress, none of us should be working here." She glanced at the somber faces and added, "We really have to do something . . . something positive."

The group squirmed uncomfortably in their chairs as Alice slowly sat down at the head of the conference table. "All right," she asked. "What are we going to do?"

The Production Manager spoke first. "I'll tell you where we should start. Tell the Purchasing Department to get us better raw materials. We can't stamp out quality products when we put junk into our machines."

"How much are you ready to pay?" the Senior Buyer responded. "We're giving you commercial quality at, I might add, very good prices. Your job is to make your people produce good product. Maybe you ought to put a little heat on your supervisors."

"Don't tell me about the cost," the Production Manger fumed. "If our customers want quality, we have to get better raw materials. That garbage you're buying is no bargain at all."

"That's right," the Quality Control Manager interjected. "Stick with quality, and in the long run our productivity will improve."

"None of us will make it to the long run," the Senior Buyer protested, "unless we get our costs down."

The Sales Manager rapped her pencil on the table, as though to demand attention. "Well, I have a problem right now. I'm sitting on a $250,000 order, and it is no good. Now I can get the customer to take it, but it'll cost us at least a 7 percent discount. Now what does TQM say we should do?"

"We have to take it back," the Quality Control Manager quickly responded. "Unless we take it back, we send a signal that we don't have a quality standard."

"Well, there is a hundred grand worth of contribution in the order. Do you want that to hit this month's P and L, Alice?"

"I want this group to quit squabbling and get down to how we improve our quality and our profits," Alice shot back, with exasperation.

The Accounting Manager felt it was time to interrupt. "With all due respect, the first priority has to be cost reduction. Our cost of getting quality is going up, not down. We are never going to make our budget if we keep going the way we are. I think we have to put TQM on the shelf for now and get after costs."

"Here we go again," the Customer Service Manager despaired. "The customer was supposed to be number one. Ha! We don't know what that means. If we can just get to the point where we give our customers the best delivery and the best quality, we'll get the orders and we'll make the profits."

"Not necessarily," said the Accounting Manager. "If we give 100 percent on-time delivery with zero defects, at costs that are too high, we'll have satisfied customers and we'll be out of business. You can't talk about quality without talking about costs."

"And you can't have those commodities without good productivity," the Production Manager added. "Every time we have a problem in the factory, we lose quality and cost. Alice, we need new equipment. QWIP showed us what we can't do. Now if you want TQM, give me some machinery so we can do things right."

"We don't have the money for new equipment," the Accounting Manager interjected. "Our ROI [return on investment] is going in the sewer, and you want to spend more money. What are we going to get for it? So far, you haven't shown any improvement in conversion cost. You can't have more capital unless your returns go up—or we'll all be out of jobs."

"We will spend money where it is necessary," Alice proclaimed. "But I agree we are not getting enough out of the machines we have. Our study of the industry proved that. Those benchmarks show we're 10–20 percent behind the competition."

"That's because we get lousy material," the Production Manager protested.

"You're getting what we can afford," the Senior Buyer countered.

"And our customers are telling us to shove it," came the Sales Manager's protest.

These comments provoked a barrage of accusations and rebuttals. When Alice regained control, she calmly rebuked the group. "This is ridiculous. We're at a crossroads here. Either we get behind the process or there will be a whole new management team. None of us seems willing to step over the threshold and make a serious commitment. Now I want you to make this happen. I will not back down. We will have Total Quality Management here. Do you understand me?"

The assembled heads nodded reluctant affirmations. Somewhere

*in the back of the room a muffled whisper summarized the atmosphere.
"Here we go again," said the anonymous voice. "We'll pretend we support TQM and our people will pretend to implement it."*

Importance of a Customized Model

When Alice Harper went in search of improvement for her
business unit, she followed most of her contemporaries. She
tried a seemingly simple lockstep methodology that was supported by documented success stories. When her achievements were followed by disappointing reversals, she became
confused and sought a different answer. Using popular theory, she then attempted to guide her people along an improvement path that had worked for other firms by empowering
her subordinates to seek their own solution. For a second time,
Alice went looking for a cookbook business recipe that would
help her organization attain goals she believed were crucial
to success and survival. On this trip, she fully expected that
higher performance would result from employing a variety
of improvement techniques selected by her own people.

   We have watched this scenario being played out across
the landscape of American business, and we analyzed the stories of these forays for improvement. What we discovered,
often by going beyond the printed word, was that *actual* results
mapped into a bell-shaped curve. On the positive side of the
curve, a few companies do achieve outstanding improvements
and move to a world-class position (our Level 3: Continuity).
Toyota, Milliken, Motorola, Emerson Electric, Xerox, and IBM-
Rochester stand out in this category. We also find organizations like Westinghouse, Caterpillar, Ford, General Motors,
and McDonnell Douglas that have business units with outstanding results. These latter firms, however, do not appear
to make similar progress across the entire organization. We
wondered why successful techniques had not worked through-

out an organization and concluded that differing local conditions and cultural circumstances mitigate against "canned approaches." The better organizations—Toyota, Milliken, Xerox, and Motorola—grew their own improvement process, using some of the better, general ideas that fit their cultures.

On the negative side of the curve, we found units, divisions, and companies that had hired some of the same people who had helped the successful firms. These organizations failed to do more than achieve momentary progress by applying the same logic and procedures espoused by the world-class organizations. In one organization we studied (a billion-dollar manufacturing firm), there were operations that had achieved 200 percent improvement in such categories as earnings, quality (measured by meaningful customer satisfaction indexes), output per employee, and product yields. Within the same company, there were an equal number of operations that had applied the same processes and had negative earnings, disgruntled customers, declining output, and poor yields.

Our conclusion from these studies is basic to achieving success with a continuous improvement effort: what works in one environment for a particular network of people, suppliers, and customers will not necessarily work in other situations. To achieve sustained success, an improvement process must fit local conditions. That means the people in the unit need to design their own improvement process so they become the *owners* of the process and assume responsibility for the results.

The opposing view reasons that faithfully following the tenets of a previously proven system should render similar, positive results. This is what most managers in our network presumed. Surely, they told us, with proper education, training, indoctrination, empowerment, and a sincere dedication to quality, productivity, and profit improvement, we should see positive results. Moreover, they argued, with virtually every U.S. firm pursuing an improvement ethic with proven principles, there should be no way our conclusion would be valid.

The results support our position. We have enough successes and nonsuccesses recorded in our portfolio to show that whatever improvement system is employed—no matter how strong the supporting logic may be, no matter how forceful the leadership mandate is, no matter how much time is spent on training, no matter how much the employees have been empowered—it had better fit the circumstances of the situation and overcome the inherent cultural obstacles, or it will not succeed. Let us cite a few examples from the failure side of our portfolio that demonstrate the folly of expecting universal success with so-called proven techniques, especially when an improvement procedure is only cosmetically endorsed by an organization.

• One firm we studied dedicated itself to a total quality improvement process with specific features related to productivity and profits. Inspired by several success stories, the managers set out to improve all facets of their business. What was missing was the necessary trust in employees to take ownership of the change process. In the prevailing culture, management legislated all changes, and the key managers refused to empower the operators and crews to build in the necessary quality improvements. Although these managers had been advised and trained to accept that such empowerment was critical for success, this group refused to let go of traditional prerogatives, and the effort failed.

• In a second example, an engineering group had designed a new product with significant advantages (they believed) over other designs in their market. Management mandated that the introduction of this innovation would be done with zero defects by making employees responsible for quality at every step in the manufacturing and service process. Unfortunately, the organization's culture did not include involving either the employees from the shop floor or the subassembly suppliers in the design phase. These groups were involved only in testing the design, which produced very questionable results. When the product hit the assembly room, in spite of pledged dedication from all employees, quality was not sustainable because of flaws in the design. Only by luck was the final assembly defect free. This company tried to impose their improvement process on a culture that gave preeminence to engineering design. The effort was doomed.

• Quite often, we find that significant progress can be made with existing capital and personnel. On those occasions when new equipment or additional personnel are necessary to gain the desired competitive advantage, a reluctance to make those investments can scuttle a well-designed improvement process. We have seen many cases where managers were reluctant to overcome their traditional propensity to withhold funds even when the results of the improvement process clearly established the need. Again, this is an example of an inappropriate fit because these managers do not understand their role in the change process.

• "Doing it right the first time" has become a rallying statement and a standard improvement cliché. The words seem to reflect sound logic. However, we have found that proponents of this approach are often left wondering: why didn't it work? We have found that people within the organization do not understand *it* or there are too many divergent opinions on *it*. We believe that the *customer* has to define *it* for the organization. If an improvement effort is foisted on a group that is not providing what the customer wants, the people get better at providing the wrong *it*. Until the proper definition of what the customer needs is developed, the fit is flawed.

• Finally, and perhaps most significant, we find the element of trust is missing from the negative end of the bell-shaped curve. When employees, suppliers, and customers do not trust each other, no improvement process will help. Each group will look for better performance from the others without being willing to put forth a similar effort. Networks of employees, suppliers, and customers must be formed before a proven improvement model can be successful.

In these situations, failure resulted from conditions *within* the organizations. Such predisposing factors should be isolated during the macro- and microanalyses of the organization's current condition, along with an examination of where the organization is, where it wants to go, and how it should go about getting there. We want to propose a strategy called *operational analysis* as a way to conduct this critical internal assessment and develop a customized operating strategy.

Operational Analysis: An Internal Assessment Procedure

There are many ways in which the internal assessment called for in Phase 2 can be performed. Outside consultants can be retained to perform an evaluation. Representatives from appropriate organizational departments can be assembled to study part or all of a business. Some combination of these groups can be formed, so the evaluation is a joint endeavor. We have used all of these procedures and have found the greatest success with an approach we call *operational analysis,* which proceeds through five steps. Basically, operational analysis is a macrolevel assessment that leads directly to improvement on a microlevel in areas identified as needing attention.

Step One: Flowchart the Process or Operation to Be Assessed

Figure 5.1 is a simple illustration of an operation that makes plastic containers. The raw materials are styrene monomer and mineral oil. The finished products are a variety of containers for use in food or food carryout packaging. The technicalities of this operation are not important for our purposes. In practice,

Figure 5.1. A Typical Flowchart.

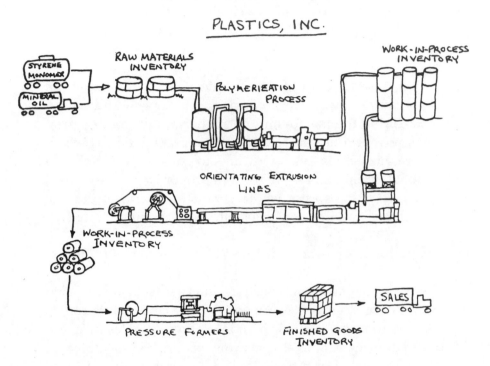

the drawing can be kept quite simple or made as elaborate as desired, without unduly delaying the analysis. Similar drawings can be made for virtually any manufacturing or service operation. A support function could also be diagrammed in terms of the functions performed. The purpose is simply to record the flow of operations so the process to be studied can be divided into segments for a team analysis. The plastic plant in our example was outlined to only include the basic operations.

Step Two: Separate the Process into Five or Six Parts

The number of parts, which is not sacrosanct, should be less than ten and more than three. The purpose of the separation is to establish subparts of the process so the analysis team will have specific areas to review. In a banking system, for example, the division could be by service provided to the customers. In Figure 5.2, the flowchart of the plastic container operation has been separated into six parts:

- Raw material receipt and storage, and polymerization (turning monomer into polymer) ("A" Sector)
- Extrusion (making a plastic sheet) and storage of work-in-process ("B" Sector)
- Thermoforming (forming containers with hot dies) ("C" Sector)
- Packaging finished goods and warehousing ("D" Sector)
- Material handling and maintenance
- Systems and procedures

Figure 5.2. A Typical Flowchart Divided for Sector Analysis.

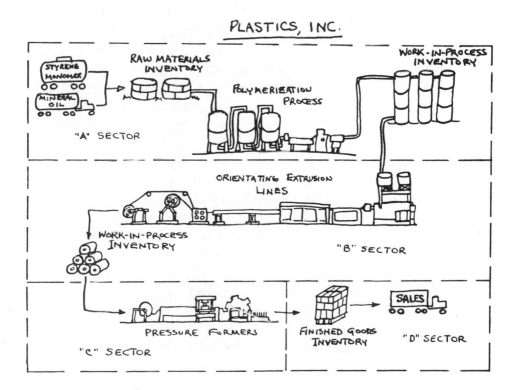

The first four sectors are marked by the dashed lines. The fifth function is plantwide, and the last function covers both plant and office. More detail can be provided, depending upon the level of understanding of the team that will be assembled. This second step establishes a plan for forming the analysis team, not to educate the members on the process. By breaking a simple—or complicated—process into five or six parts, people with the appropriate skills can be selected to make an analysis in a defined area. For a service organization lacking in-house experts, use of outside consultants can produce the desired results, but care should be exercised in the flowchart segmentation to get the most benefit from this more expensive expertise.

Step Three: Form an Analysis Team

With the operation divided into study areas, a search is made for a two-individual team for each section. The intent is to find people qualified to make a quick, but meaningful, assessment of what is happening in each section and then explain their findings lucidly to the resident manager of the operation. For example, the individuals considered for the raw material sector (Sector A) should know about the characteristics of monomer, how it should be transported and stored, and how the basic polymerization process takes place. Their depth of knowledge should be such that, if necessary, they could operate or supervise the functions in Sector A. Those selected for the thermoforming section (Section C) should know materials, machinery, and the manufacturing process. The systems and procedures team (Sector F) should know the overall process and be current on state-of-the-art information processing. In short, we want to assemble two experts per sector with such skills that when they enter the prescribed area and begin their analysis, those working in the area will readily appreciate their expertise. They should also have the ability to interview both hourly and salaried people and translate their findings into a lucid evaluation of what is happening (including a discussion of the cultural attitudes toward change).

The source of these teams can be operators, supervisors, or technicians from similar plants. They can come from technical support groups, machinery manufacturers, suppliers, or retired veterans still familiar with the operation. They can be sales representatives or office personnel. The major qualification is the ability to diagnose the true output of the operation under analysis. These individuals must be able to filter the positive inputs from involved managers to determine the reality of what is happening and the true feelings about doing things differently.

When formed, the team for our food-packaging operation will consist of twelve individuals, or experts, who are prepared to objectively analyze the operation to determine its state of preparation for a continuous improvement effort. Obviously, the techniques—and team—are useful for evaluating the current performance of an operation. If the unit being studied is on multiple shifts, the team size should double.

Step Four: Study the Operation

For a period of two days, the team observes the operation. The ground rules are quite simple:

- *Catch people doing things right; catch people doing things wrong.* Even the poorest operator has some good practices that should be passed on to similar operations. It is essential to seek positive attributes as well as negative to avoid the accusation that the analysis was simply a witch-hunt intended to find faults. An easy way to express this instruction to the team is to tell them to find "the good, the bad, and the ugly." The *good* is a practice that should be duplicated at similar operations. The *bad* is something that should be improved. The *ugly* should be improved immediately, for example, an unsafe practice that could cause injury.

- *Talk first to the hourly personnel; then to the salaried personnel.*
  The purpose of the analysis is to find out, quickly, what
  is truly happening so the operation can prepare to implement positive changes. If a false impression is created
  by salaried personnel fearful of the impact of negative
  findings, then the exercise will be a waste. The team has
  to start with dialogue between themselves and the people
  most familiar with daily operations—those who create the
  product or provide the service under observation. In a
  service operation, where all employees might be salaried,
  discretion should be used to separate the workers from
  the managers. The analyst needs both perspectives on
  what is happening.

The two-person teams study their area of inspection and
discuss what they see with the people performing the work.
Then they proceed to discuss their observations with—or seek
more information from—the supervisors and managers. It
should be apparent why two people are put on each section
of the team. They form a minipanel to field the responses of
the salaried personnel, some of which can be expected to be
in conflict with information received from the rank-and-file
personnel. They also have the chance to discuss between themselves what they think is the reality of the situation and where
potentially beneficial alliances can be created.

Step Five: Present Observations to the Resident Manager

Toward the end of the second day, the resident manager will
assemble his or her direct reports, and the analysis team will
make a verbal presentation of the findings. A written report
can be made to document the findings, but we must offer a
caution. Since negative results can be expected, the possibility
that a party responsible for the nonperformance will be sought
is great. This matter should be handled by the resident manager. Written reports have a way of getting the bad news—

without any mitigating good news—to higher authority. We have had great success by keeping the operational analysis and any documentation within the confines of the unit being studied. In that way, future analyses of other operations is easier because improvements have been made without the typical personnel displacement. Necessary changes are accomplished, but the witch-hunt syndrome is avoided.

Operational analysis is one way to conduct an internal assessment. It is not the final step nor is it the only technique available. We have also used industrial engineering teams, joint support group-line teams, and combination consultant–support group–line groups. The advantage of the operational analysis approach is the involvement of many people from across the organization, who then become interested in the results of the assessment and want to participate at other locations. We definitely would have recommended this procedure to Alice as one way to force an internal assessment inside her house. It would have helped her determine which units were in order and ready to pursue continuous improvement and which needed some repairs and an infusion of partnering before proceeding.

Other variations of this technique can be used. The point remains the same. Some system must be used to isolate the issues, opportunities, and problems that stand between current performance and best-in-class status. The analysis also has to put on the table for confrontation and resolution the obstacles and cultural inhibitors that will reduce the possibility of success.

Benchmarking

Benchmarking is the setting of stretch targets for performance based on the best performances within an industry or profession. William Camp (1979) of Xerox Corporation developed the term at a time when Xerox was concerned with a severe loss of competitive position. He defined benchmarking as the "continuous process of measuring our products, services and practices against our toughest competitors or those companies recognized as industry leaders" (p. 10). By 1981, the technique was in corporatewide use at Xerox, which used what it learned from the procedure to regain and sustain a leadership position in its marketplace.

Benchmarking can be extremely useful as the improvement model is fitted to the organization or unit's specific circumstances. After the macro- and microanalyses are completed, the information gathered should be used in establishing benchmarks for the organization; progress has to begin with a solid understanding of where the business is starting, which should be provided by the analyses. We extend the definition of benchmarking to include units *within* an organization as a starting point. In that way, we establish both an internal and external benchmark.

A recent experience of ours is useful in illustrating how benchmarking works. When asked to introduce an improvement process to a newly acquired subsidiary organization, we began by comparing the subsidiary's current performance against clearly similar operations within the parent firm. The average of the similar units was established as the beginning internal benchmark. We discovered that performance of the subsidiary was 20 percent below that level, and the initial target was set to exceed that benchmark. By questioning the managers on their ability to reach the target, we found a significant negative attitude in a key manager. This individual did not believe it was possible for the subsidiary to be that far below any average performance or that it was possible to make the targeted improvement. This manager's full support was essential to the process, so further effort was delayed until a real commitment was forthcoming. It required some convincing arguments and inspection of higher-performing units, but the manager's support was finally achieved.

As the subsidiary neared the internal benchmark, reliable

industry data reflecting the performance of the best manufacturers of the same product line were collected by members of the subsidiary. This data became the external benchmark—the best of the best. Performances were compared on such measures as:

- Productivity per hour
- On-time deliveries
- Product yield or waste
- Transactions per employee
- Quality levels, warranty costs

It was possible to establish the gap between the subsidiary and the best-performing competitors. It was also possible to ascertain the reactions of the key managers. This feedback provided invaluable insights into the cultural inhibitions that had to be overcome if the improvement process was to succeed. Our logical next step became dealing with those complications before wasting time and energies on something that was doomed to fail.

Benchmarking expected or targeted performance at levels consistent with what competition is already achieving is a powerful tool for motivating greater performance. When those within the organization believe in the validity of the benchmarks, they have little choice but to pursue the higher levels of performance. Some negative responses can be expected from managers who will insist on denying the accuracy of the benchmarks or defending their performance with myriad excuses. Generally, this opposition subsides, and the group proceeds in search of the new level of performance. To fail to do this is tantamount to accepting a going-out-of business posture as the better competitor continues to enlarge the performance gap. Eventually, dedicated groups will pass the internal benchmarks and proceed toward the external marks.

The real purpose behind the employment of benchmarking is to find the best practice or technique, that is, the best way of performing a function, in order to attain world-class status for an organization. Benchmarking numbers and data are useful guides to where superior performance must proceed. Tables 2.1 and 2.2 (p. 21 and pp. 23–24) display the qualities of excellent performers, and we would like to remind readers that these characteristics are the goals of benchmarking.

A natural question regarding internal and external benchmarking is, how does one capture the pertinent data? There are a variety of sources. Trade journals and industry publications are a valuable source. We suggest first visiting the company or local business library. Clever people sent on a search for comparative data generally find far more useful information than might be expected. Such people are also capable of preparing surveys that may elicit surprising information from carefully selected respondents. Outside consultants and students can also be used to gather data.

Our most successful technique has been direct contact with organizations we believe are the best at a particular function. Another source of data on a specific competitor is mutual suppliers of machinery and materials. There are many techniques available, and as experience is gained, the accuracy of the data collected will amaze the organizations interested in pursuing the top performers.

Improvement Tools

After the analyses have been completed and benchmarks established, what techniques – or tools – are available and effective for the execution component of Phase 2 of the continuous improvement model? How can they be customized to fit a specific situation? We propose a menu-like listing of effective tools, with managers and facilitators choosing those techniques that most reasonably match the needs of the particular circumstance. In this sense, the improvement model is applied in a customized manner, fitting the correct

Figure 5.3. Improvement Tools.

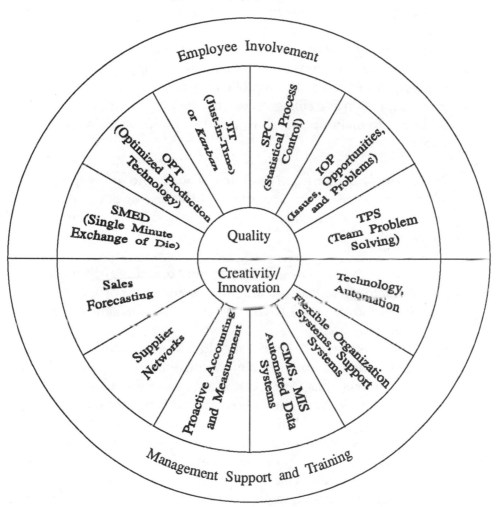

improvement approach to the appropriate issue. Figure 5.3 depicts a model of the type of menus that will make continuous improvement work. This model consists of three rings, similar to the major aspects of the improvement model, that must operate as a consistent system to be useful and effective.

Outer Ring: Management Support
and Employee Involvement

The outer ring contains two elements essential to success with any improvement endeavor. Management support must be logically combined with employee involvement so the two groups function as a cohesive, partnering unit. Both elements will have to make special contributions if improvement is to work.

Management Support and Training. Those who are responsible for overseeing the operations of the organization must supply certain key elements to make the improvement effort successful:

- The central purposes, objectives, and business goals must be stated in a clear and articulate manner. If participants do not understand where the effort is going, the effort will fail.
- The direction of the effort should take—including a clear delineation of subordinate responsibilities, timetables, and targets—has to be worked out in a series of meetings involving leaders and subordinates. It is here that any potential withholding of support by managers should be isolated and addressed. All constituencies must have a sense of ownership of the developed plans.
- A communication system to report progress must be designed and put into place. There should be an on-going reporting process that keeps the participants aware of how the gap between where they started and where they are going is being closed. This is like watching an athletic contest; without a scoreboard it is hard to follow whether your team is winning or losing.
- Resources required to facilitate the improvement processes have to be provided, and without slowing the process through incessant negotiations. This means that

senior managers provide the necessary resources, matched to the needs of the improvement effort and the payback for the investment. Then the teams get on with the improvement effort.

- Training in any area where those involved are less than fully capable is designed and carried out.

Employee Involvement. The workers, in response to managers who no longer treat them as though they had checked their brains at the entrance to the workplace, will provide these essential inputs:

- The development of work systems and procedures that have been redesigned to be more meaningful and effective. Redundancy will be eliminated. Team elements will be introduced to improve flow and make the work more rewarding. Self-regulation can easily become a part of this development as the labor-management alliance designs the work to reflect trust in employees and sets up shared rewards for the effort.
- The commitment to accomplishing the specific targets, outlined in clear direction statements. Now the sense of continuous improvement, or what the Japanese call *kaizen* (Imai, 1986), can flow from the bottom as well as the top of the organization.
- Through increased training and support, workers will gain a deeper understanding of the organization, which will allow them to challenge the status quo and build more effective systems.
- The excellence of job performance that ensures each individual is doing his or her personal best.

Center Ring: Twelve Techniques

The center ring contains twelve of the most appropriate techniques to bring continuous improvement to an organization.

There are others that could be listed. The ones shown in Figure 5.3 have been our most effective tools. Two factors prompt us to present so many of these techniques: (1) we have rarely seen a single tool bring the kind of significant short- and long-term improvement that most managers seek and (2) most evidence from our success stories indicates that multiple systems are necessary to achieve success in an environment as complicated and dynamic as a modern organization. Using a menu-like approach, the manager—who has analyzed an operation and is aware of the current cultural obstacles—can select the appropriate tools for the identified issues. The idea is to offer multiple selections to empowered employees, who will accept responsibility for achieving targeted purposes.

The twelve sections of the recommended menu are divided into two parts: the alphabet soup of techniques that engender improvement and the support systems that management must supply to reinforce the achievement.

Alphabet Soup of Improvement Procedures

1. *SMED* (Single Minute Exchange of Die): the Shigeo Shingo (1985) technique of dividing setup and changeover into external and internal elements and concentrating on reducing the internal time so the machine is down during changeover for the minimum time. This tool encourages belief in the power of crew participation, as setups typically improve by 2X or 5X.

2. *OPT* (Optimized Production Technology): the Eliyahu Goldratt (1984) technique of planning and controlling processing so throughput is raised while simultaneously cutting inventories and operating expenses. This tool is extremely useful in highlighting the parts of the system that control throughput and making certain improvement resources are focused on the right *it*.

3. *JIT* (Just-in-Time or *Kanban*): the Taiichi Ohno (1986) technique of reducing waste through procedures that estab-

lish communications throughout the production process to ensure that all resources are optimally used.

4. *SPC* (Statistical Process Control): the technique popularized by W. Edwards Deming (1982) to isolate the controllable aspects in a process from the random variation, through use of statistical analysis. With correct information, the crews establish control within acceptable ranges through manual or automatic monitoring and adjustment. This tool allows hourly employees to be involved in gathering data on their part of the process. They learn to isolate what controls output, which leads to improvements of their own design.

5. *IOP* (Issues, Opportunities, and Problems): a technique we developed to draw out the salient opportunities for improvement through team processing. This procedure involves developing a prioritized list of current improvement opportunities, based on what should be done in the next six months, six months to one year, and over a year.

6. *TPS* (Team Problem Solving): the technique popularized by Joseph Juran and others that uses team actions to resolve opportunities on a project-by-project basis. This tool helps reluctant managers accept the concepts of the improvement effort because it gets them involved in accepting recommendations on problems they know need resolving.

Management Support Systems

1. *Sales Forecasting:* a crucial element to make planning, inventory control, scheduling, servicing, and delivery function in an efficient and effective manner.

2. *Supplier Networks:* using suppliers who can deliver—on time and at competitive costs—the quality goods and services necessary to ensure production of goods or services of the highest possible quality. Included in this network are suppliers who will work diligently as active partners to seek extra value through the relationship.

3. *Proactive Accounting and Measurement:* this is a crucial function that goes beyond traditional accounting procedures to measure performance and motivate progress in terms easily understood by all participants. This tool is also necessary to get the active participation of the financial group in the improvement effort.
4. *CIMS, MIS, Automated Data Systems:* computer-integrated management systems, management information systems, and so on must be part of a system to provide accurate and timely data and review on a daily basis.
5. *Flexible Organization Systems, Support Systems:* matrix arrangements, compensatory tie-ins with improvement performance, specialized "corrective action" teams, and other visible supports are crucial to effectively demonstrate management's continued interest and support of the improvement process. The recruitment and reward systems must be challenged to make certain they are truly supportive of the mission statement and the type of alliances that are forged with all constituencies.
6. *Technology, Automation:* new systems and machinery are important factors, so it is critical that the company be sufficiently state-of-the-art. Better equipped competitors could gain an insurmountable advantage.

There are three caveats that should be observed:

- *Maintain a customer orientation.* The complete improvement system has to be market driven. At all times, the goal should be to promote the satisfaction of customer needs — both internally and externally. To do otherwise is to build an efficient system that has no utility.
- *Remember the Pareto Principle* (that is, in most situations, 80 percent of the opportunities for improvement come from 20 percent of the problems or issues under consideration). Prioritize issues, opportunities, and problems. Then concentrate on the vital few issues that will capture

people's attention and provide for the kinds of returns that will ensure the continuation of the process. Avoid the many trivial problems that only sap time and energies.

- *Instill the attitude that the job is never done.* Improvement has to be a continuous procedure, not a quick fix. As soon as one set of resources is approaching optimization, the manager should select another opportunity. New objectives should be introduced as old ones are attained, and the process repeated—again and again.

Inner Ring: Quality and Creativity

The inner ring shows the dual requirements of quality and creativity/innovation. Quality must be reflected in all jobs performed within the company. Every employee has to be convinced that doing one's personal best is crucial to everyone's survival. Our favorite technique is to use a large process map, or flowchart, of the total network to illustrate to all employees how vital each job performance is to total success. Stepping through such a chart enables individuals to see what can happen when their part of the flow is off-quality. Innovation helps maintain a competitive pace, and new ideas and their application become central. These two attributes—quality and creativity/innovation—must characterize all twelve procedures as well as the employee and management actions depicted in the outer ring.

The First Requirement: A House in Order

If we return to the heroine of our story, we realize that Alice is still facing a dilemma. In spite of substantial hours spent pursuing what must have looked to be a simple way to make progress, her unit has done nothing more than tread water. At this stage, her organization is most likely demoralized in every sector, and she is under pressure to show better results. Unless she can pull the unit together and get an improvement system that everyone accepts, her results—and her career—are doomed.

Alice has a model for implementation, with benchmarked targets as goals. She certainly knows at this point that the process is harder to implement than expected. Her key managers have yet to comprehend the role they must play in achieving success. There are no alliances at their level: they are each chasing separate agendas. The brief moment when they collectively developed their improvement model has faded from memory. Their disoriented actions are confusing the employees. Instead of fostering progress, they collectively have created a business mess. Many organizations faced with similar circumstances simply give up at this point and focus on traditional cost-reduction programs. When the managers of such firms look over their shoulders to review their results, they see the recommended ingredients for a successful effort. What they do not see is that they failed to put their house in order before applying those sound improvement techniques.

Alice's dilemma has been experienced by many firms, large and small. John R. Anderluh (1990), president and CEO of Moore Business Forms, North American Operations, reported on his organization's improvement project. In Moore's case, the quest was for Total Quality Management (TQM). Managers started by attending conferences, reading books, and reviewing research articles. Their first conclusion was that the process seemed easy. Their subsequent struggles proved the fallacy of that initial conclusion. Moore has finally obtained their objectives, but Anderluh now admits that they should have begun with an external evaluation to define quality from the consumer's viewpoint before trying to make improvements. As he says, "How can you improve if the person you want to satisfy hasn't told you where you are?" We would add: without an assessment of where you are versus someone who is better, key managers do not see the need for a tough journey to a higher position.

To reap the benefits of continuous improvement and business partnering, an organization has to be ready, mentally and physically, to implement the changes that will result in the desired improvements. Assuring such preparedness requires an organization to begin internally with an honest assessment of current performance. External information on what the customer wants can help guide the assessment, but the key is to determine the mind-set of essential participants to anticipate what will help and hinder successful implementation. An evaluation should be made of total resources (the purpose being to determine the organization's strengths and weaknesses) and, more important, of the cultural inhibitions that will affect the necessary change process. Finally, the positive aspects of the culture are used as the foundation of an orderly house, with meaningful alliances throughout the organization becoming the pillars that support the house.

Action Study: Toyota Motor Corporation

Toyota came into existence in 1937, when the Toyoda family of Japan began manufacturing automobiles. The early times were not marked by great success; in the first thirteen years of its existence, Toyota produced less than 3,000 cars. Today, Toyota ranks as one of the leading automakers in the world in terms of quality, productivity, profit, and customer service. The company has experienced great success in the U.S. car market. What Toyota has accomplished provides a model of what can be achieved when an enlightened leadership utilizes the precepts of what we call business partnering with sincerity and continuous dedication.

Partnering between potentially antagonistic parties began for Toyota when a very special agreement was reached with its union. Under the terms of that pact, employees are guaranteed lifetime employment, with a pay scale that escalates with years of service. To gain this concession from the company, members of the union agreed to be flexible regarding work assignments and to help the firm find new and improved methods for increasing productivity, quality, and profits. The parties might not have considered their alliance a form of partnering, but the results have been exactly what can happen when a pact favors both sides.

Toyota's arrangement has been a win-win situation. With their landmark agreement, union and management went to work together seeking to gain a leadership position in the automobile industry. Their target—what we have been calling the external benchmark—became the leading U.S. carmakers—Ford and General Motors. Toyota's relentless pursuit has paid great dividends in terms of market share and profitability.

A second partnership was forged internally between Eiji Toyoda, a member of the founding family, and Taiichi Ohno, the head of Toyota operations—an individual destined to leave an indelible mark on Japanese and American manufacturing systems. Together they set out to study American and European car manufacturing techniques. After lengthy evaluations, they concluded that what had worked in the United States for decades—*mass producing units for inventory* and selling through an obliging dealer network to consumers happy to get an automobile—would not work in Japan or survive in the future world market. This conclusion led them to launch a revolutionary methodology in automaking. Under Ohno's watchful guidance, Toyota worked on dramatically reducing the time required to produce a car, in order to switch from an orientation of having cars in inventory to one of producing cars to meet customer demands. From this new philosophy have come quality, productivity, and inventory improvements that have seeped into all modern efforts.

Beginning with quality, Ohno reasoned that it was wrong to have mistakes occur. Since the worker controlled how each job was performed, the worker had to control mistakes. The worker had to make quality a reality. Quality was not defined as zero defects. It was defined as building the very best and giving the customer what was wanted. To build with zero defects could create perfect cars without the features wanted by the customer. More important, the emphasis should be on delighting the customer. In this latter aspect, Ohno reasoned that customers should never be told they had to wait for a new car. The car should be made to order and delivered in a reasonable time. To accomplish these ends, the manufacturing system had to be more flexible, respond faster, and produce no mistakes.

To facilitate these concepts, Ohno, in cooperation with many others who worked in the Toyota system, originated such practices as:

- *Kanban:* delivery of parts when needed in the quantity needed
- *JIT:* just-in-time manufacture and delivery, an extension of *kanban* that results in the correct product or services being created just-in-time for intended use, with zero waste in the process
- *Andon:* the use of display boards that immediately show a problem in any part of the assembly process, so remedial action can be focused quickly in that area

Through a further alliance with Shigeo Shingo, a Japanese consultant and expert on rapid change techniques, they contributed these concepts:

- *SMED.* single minute exchange of dies, the technique for reducing changeover times, often from hours to minutes
- *Poka-Yoke:* the means by which improvements are built into the process and foolproofed so the gains are sustained

These contributions form a significant legacy for one organization to pass on. Toyota truly employed business partnering to foster quality, productivity, and profit improvement in a holistic manner. A study of Toyota's evolution reveals that it stressed all three elements simultaneously to satisfy customers and gain a competitive advantage. An early example occurred when Ohno used a transformation of a simple formula to bring focus to the factor of cost. The traditional formula for determining selling price is:

Selling Price = Cost + Profit

Under the terms of this formula, the cost of producing a product or service is developed, the desired profit is added to the cost, and the sum is used as the selling price—assuming the market will allow it.

The transformation made by Ohno was to cast the formula as:

Profit = Selling Price − Cost

Ohno assumed that price was determined by the marketplace. Certainly, in the early days of Toyota, other manufacturers could establish selling prices far more definitively than could a small Japanese firm. Under this transformed concept, to make a reasonable profit the only recourse was to lower the cost as much as possible. Thus began Ohno's and Toyota's relentless pursuit of the lowest cost. A saying of Ohno that captures this philosophy is, "True cost is only the size of a plum seed." He determined that a problem with most managers was their tendency to inflate the plum seed into a "huge grapefruit." They then shave off some unevenness from the rind and call it cost reduction. "How wrong can they get?" he asked.

Some of Toyota's results have been truly spectacular. Working with Shingo and his SMED techniques in 1970, Toyota determined it took four hours to exchange a particular die for a 1,000-ton stamping press. By investigating other company practices, it found that Volkswagen could change a similar die in two hours (an external benchmark). Within six months, Toyota had reduced the changeover to one and a half hours. Three months later, the order came to reduce the time to three minutes. Toyota eventually reduced the time to one minute, four seconds.

Toyota discovered that SMED had utility beyond reducing die exchange time. A decision was made to become proficient at small-lot production to eliminate the waste from overproduction and to become more customer responsive. The reasoning was that the briefer the time necessary to make a changeover, the shorter would be the time necessary to deliver what the customer wanted, rather than making the customer select from inventory. To meet these goals, SMED was absolutely essential. *Kanban* then became the controlling mechanism to move the correct amount of product through the Toyota manufacturing system. *Poka-Yoke* was added to foolproof the system in order to prevent careless mistakes that create customer dissatisfaction.

The JIT concept probably originated in Japanese ship-building at a time when steel companies had greatly increased their supply capacities. In their hunger for orders, these steelmakers began delivering product just-in-time from their extra inventories. Ohno, true to the Japanese culture, credits the use of the term *just-in-time* to another member of the founding family, Kiichiro Toyoda, the first president of Toyota. Whatever the origin, Ohno moved the idea from concept to practice. Under his direction, *Kanban* became "let the process that needs parts go to get what is needed, when needed, in the quantity needed."

Ohno eventually built the entire production process around JIT. His aim was to manufacture only what was needed, when needed, in the amount needed. His technique was simple. An empty container was returned to a supplying machine as the signal to turn out more parts. Inventories shrank close to zero. The small problems that could disrupt the manufacturing system were eliminated because everyone had to focus on solving the problems for good; so the small problems no longer existed. Ohno replaced Henry Ford's *mass production* with what Toyota terms *lean production,* a far more efficient and higher-quality methodology. He put the final touches on the process when he decreed the "essence" of the Toyota system to be the total elimination of waste:

- Waste from overproducing
- Waste from waiting time
- Waste from transporting
- Waste from processing
- Waste from unnecessary inventory
- Waste from unnecessary motion
- Waste from producing defective goods

Using the concept (becoming more accepted in the United States) that labor costs were as fixed as other overhead items, Ohno determined to continuously improve worker ability and to tap workers' concepts and ideas for improvement. Using the seven categories of waste as the primary target, he organized his workers into teams and instructed them to determine the best way to do the necessary work to produce a car. Over time, the teams' responsibilities were enlarged to include minor maintenance and quality checks. At all times, they studied ways and sought the means to improve the process and the end product.

Often, the improvement techniques were very simple. Ohno placed red handles at each work station, with the instruction that if a problem occurred, employees were to stop the assembly line, trace the problem to its root cause, and fix it so it would not happen again. Initially, the assembly line was interrupted frequently. Ohno persevered. The line ran more continuously because errors decreased. Today, there are virtually no rework areas. Yields approach 100 percent, and the lines run continuously.

Under Toyota's version of partnering, 73 percent of parts are supplied by outside vendors (versus 30 percent for General Motors). Toyota established the price it can pay to its partnering suppliers. Then Toyota and its suppliers work together to determine how a car (and components) can be assembled for that price and allow both parties to make a reasonable profit. Under this system, cost savings initiated by the supplier go to the supplier.

The overall results of the Toyota system include reduced costs per unit, improved quality, and more rapid response to customers. Toyota can produce a luxury sedan with one-sixth the labor required for more expensive German units. Cost per unit has been consistently under that of American manufacturers. Toyota has the highest operating margin in the automobile industry and can build-to-order in seven to ten days, versus the normal months quoted in the United States.

Toyota, in alliance with workers and suppliers, is setting most of the benchmarks in the auto manufacturing industry. Its quest is for sustained competitive advantage as it builds the best quality at the lowest cost. Toyota's is truly a continuous improvement effort that has attained the third level of success.

Summary

In this chapter, we have argued for the importance of this principle: improvement efforts that work in one organization will not necessarily work in others. An improvement process must fit local conditions. It is critical, therefore, that an improvement effort include an in-depth analysis—at both macro- and microlevels—to isolate the problems and issues that could impede success and to highlight the reality of an organization's operations.

We recommend the use of benchmarking to establish targets that have meaning for an organization's particular circumstances and have outlined tools to aid in the implementation of successful results. We believe that an organization should put its own house in order before proceeding externally, and in the next chapter, we examine barriers to progress of a truly internal nature.

Chapter Six

◆

How To
Overcome Obstacles

The internal assessment discussed in Chapter Five is invaluable in developing the necessary road map for the improvement journey. It also points out the cultural barriers that will slow the progress of the trip. Many of these barriers have been discussed. What remains to be considered are those of a truly local nature. We refer to the personal attitudes, concerns, and traditional power positions that make it difficult for managers to make the most of a process intended to benefit the entire organization.

The purpose of this chapter is to illustrate how to overcome this resistance, which is usually never verbalized. First, we want to visit with Alice Harper once more. This time we watch as she tries to get to the root cause of her unit's nonperformance.

Alice Faces the Real Enemy

Bothered by the feedback and the negative reactions from her performance appraisals, Alice decided to conduct a series of interviews with each manager of her unit. The first of these interviews was with the Sales Manager. After assuring her that the purpose was to determine how to make more progress with the improvement effort and not to look for a scapegoat, Alice stated that she wanted to focus on the issues as viewed from the sales perspective.

"As I see it," the Sales Manager postulated, "you never got a clear message across to the Production Department. We still have late deliveries, our promise of JIT shipments fell through, my reps are embarrassed to talk about orders missing specs, and you should see the way they pack the trailers. I mean, it didn't happen. We've had the meetings. We agreed with the program. Maybe you have the wrong people leading this thing. They talk a good game, but they can't execute."

"Have you done your part?" Alice asked. "Has the Sales Department made its contribution?"

"What's that supposed to mean?" she responded. "Yes, we've done our job. We always do our job. We went to the customers with what we were trying to do. We got their input into what it means to have good specs. The production group messed up. That's what it amounts to."

Alice spread some papers in front of the Sales Manager. "According to this data, over one-third of all orders entered by your sales force have at least two errors. Since we process sixty orders a day, that means on average we are putting through at least forty bad specifications per day. That isn't the fault of the production department. That's the responsibility . . . "

"Where did you get that data?" the Sales Manager interrupted. "Who says we have that many errors? The Accounting Department?"

"We pulled out the orders for last month," replied Alice, "to see if we had achieved quality in the order entry process. We haven't. I had the orders gone over and any error was circled. These are the facts."

"I don't know how that can be," was the Sales Manager's excuse. "There is no way we are putting that many mistakes into the system. It has to be the Customer Service group. They could screw up anything."

"Apparently, Customer Service has been trying to cover for the Sales Department for a long time," Alice remarked coolly. "It seems that three or four of your best representatives refuse to use the order entry forms. They submit all incoming sales data by hand, usually on loose sheets from a tablet."

"What's wrong with that?" asked the Sales Manager. "They get the orders. That's what counts."

"What is wrong," Alice replied, "is that they all flunked Palmer penmanship! You can't read their writing, so the people in Customer Service have to guess at the specifications."

"Look," the Sales Manager fumed. "Do you want orders or good penmanship?"

"I want accuracy," Alice replied calmly. "And I want discipline. Now if you can't get your people to do things right, tell me. Tell me now, so I can find someone who will."

The conversation with the Production Manager started on a similarly defensive note. Following a question by Alice as to why the shop floor data had deteriorated in accuracy, he replied, "I am not aware of any problems. I thought we got that issue straightened out when the new Accounting Manager showed up."

"We ran a check on last month's reports," Alice said. "It seems there has been considerable backsliding. The shop floor information is in error over 40 percent of the time . . . not by much, in most cases . . . but enough to make the productivity analysis next to worthless."

"What are you talking about?" he protested. "That information comes right from the factory production reports. The entries have to be approved by the supervisors."

"I know," Alice interrupted. "And when we started a push on setup times, they simply allowed the operators to record lower amounts to make it look like we were making progress. The fact is, we have paid awards to crews where there has been no real improvement."

"I don't know how that can be," the Production Manager protested. "Who gave you this information? Those bean counters in Accounting?"

"It doesn't matter who told me," Alice responded directly. "The fact is you have allowed the reporting system to be corrupted. We're supposed to run a business, and we have no idea what our real costs are."

"It's not as bad as that," the Production Manager said with a feigned grin. "We can't be off more than a few percent."

"The issue is not percent of error," Alice retorted. "You agreed to see that reporting was accurate, and it has actually gotten worse."

The Customer Service Manager sat on the edge of his chair as Alice probed into details of contacts between the service correspondents and customers.

"It seems your people have been adding a day or two to every delivery promise made to the customer," Alice remarked, pointing to some data sheets.

"They do . . . on occasion," came the Customer Service Manager's reply. "We can't trust the accuracy of the shop floor information. Unless we follow each order, we never really know where the product is. By adding a day or two, the customer gets the product on time or even ahead of schedule."

"That makes a mess out of the system," Alice rebuked. "There is no integrity in what we are doing."

"Look," he replied cautiously. "My department deals directly with the customer. They can get product from four or five competitors. Our job is to keep the order. If we fudge the information a little, it is for our own good."

" We will never improve the delivery system," Alice corrected, "if we keep adding slack to cover inadequacies."

"We add what we need to keep the customer happy," the Customer Service Manager responded. "When we see the production group start to deliver on time, then we will quote the right delivery."

The Accounting Manager went on the attack. "Yes, I know our reports have errors in them. We get tired of waiting for the numbers to come in right. My people are worn out from all the overtime needed to get the figures to show what really happened. Unless we accept some of the garbage we get, there would be no closing."

The Quality Control Manager was apathetic. "We had a great meeting. We put a lot of problems on the table . . . and I thought we had consensus. I was genuinely excited by the plan we developed."

"What went wrong?" Alice asked.

"The key people . . . the managers who agreed to the plan . . . were never on board," was her reply. "We went back to work and that plan lasted a few months . . . no more. As soon as one of the managers had to do more than business as usual, they started to lose their interest. We never did have an agreement or any consensus. We're all interested in our own agenda. The plan looked like it would help, but no one was ready for any sacrifice . . . or any recognition that they were part of the problem."

"When the plan was presented to me," Alice said, "the names of all the managers were on it."

"I know," was the Quality Control Manager's weak response. "We all signed it, but no one meant it. We thought it was the thing to do.

We did have a plan that made sense, but no one was prepared to sacrifice anything to make it happen. We all wanted someone else to make the improvements. I guess in a way, we had it in our heads . . . but not in our hearts."

Alice held several other discussions. They confirmed that in no part of the business unit had the full intentions of the improvement process been implemented. Some savings and a few changes had been enacted, but the overall results were right where they had been the previous year. Alice was not sure at this point if any real progress had been made. She knew the dilemma had not passed, and her career hopes were dimming. She was also convinced she now knew the real enemy. She knew she had no true alliances among her managers that would ensure the success she so desperately sought. For a long time, she sat at her desk considering whether or not to continue the effort.

Characteristics of Successful Implementation

We have discussed disoriented leadership and tubular thinking as obstacles to successful implementation. We have also mentioned the problems that result from jumping for a quick fix, expecting great results from a single focus, using lockstep improvement processes, and not custom fitting the improvement effort to local conditions. With these limitations in mind, we want to move on to discuss how to overcome complications so that continuous improvement will succeed.

There are many complications to execution of a continuous improvement effort. Our experience has taught us, repeatedly, that the probability of significant improvement increases if the following four characteristics are present:

The Group at the Top Functions as a Cohesive Unit

The word *team* is probably overused, but it is a critical concept for the small, senior group responsible for creating, developing, introducing, adjusting, monitoring, and supporting the improvement process. When the operational gap has been defined by the macro- and microanalyses and benchmarks have been established, the natural tendency is to launch an intense effort to close the gap and gain an advantage. Senior officers typically charge forward, expecting committed employees to follow. This has occurred in Alice Harper's group.

The better approach is to take the time to develop a strong consensus and the necessary supporting features at the top before beginning an improvement effort in the ranks. We prefer to take the senior group to an off-site locale and spend whatever time is necessary to talk the issues through until there is near-total acceptance of the process intentions, scope of actions, necessary cultural changes, rewards and recognitions, supporting systems, and the details of how managers must enact their part of the mission statement. The alternative is disorientation and a sad medley of differing versions of how to execute the same improvement effort.

What can happen when there is no real acceptance of the impending changes is illustrated by what happened when Japanese manufacturers attempted to run facilities within the United States using their strongly people-oriented techniques. Many American managers who agreed to adopt the recommended practices, which included heavy doses of employee idea generation and team decision making, were unable to execute those practices. The reasons are basic to the U.S. business culture; managers do not usually trust employees to execute with such responsibility, and the sharing of credit for success runs against the normal management orientation.

Management Models the Correct Role

When consensus is reached on how the group at the top will function as a cohesive unit, the individuals within that unit have to get out of their offices and "walk the talk." That phrase has come into popular use to mean to go among the people who are part of the execution network and model the role that will inspire successful execution of the process. Memoranda, a periodic call, a video or faxed message will not suffice. Personal contact is the only way to reinforce that everyone's orientation will stay focused on the basic issues and that managers throughout the organization will set aside their silos and work with suppliers, customers, and employees to make the effort a mutual success.

Proper execution of this technique is invaluable. Direct contact provides for the elimination of typical filtering of unpleasant data (the unwillingness of subordinates to relay information on problems to their boss, in the hopes they can make improvement before the boss decides they have been part of the problem), discovery of the real rate of progress, and contact with a *role model to follow and execute against* for the people closest to the areas needing improvement. These people respond well to such modeling, and the positive feedback they give to the senior manager taking the time to walk the talk can be very rewarding—for both parties.

*The Improvement Effort Is Started
When the Troops Are Ready*

Most failures in our portfolio have a similar characteristic; improvement efforts were begun prematurely, before the understanding and sincere support of key personnel had been achieved. These false starts leave organizations with disillusioned and apathetic employees, who simply await the next "flavor of the month"—the newest improvement fad to be foisted on them.

If an improvement process is under way (which is true for most business organizations) and results are failing to meet desired objectives, this point is critical. Those leading the effort should regroup, develop a clearer road map that will gain acceptance from key constituents, and then follow that route as they chase stretch objectives. This means that groups within the firm, with assistance from suppliers and customers, have to rethink, in a frank and open way, what is working and what is failing.

Those portions of the organization that are not meeting objectives usually have very precise reasons for nonimplementation. The tendency is to ignore those circumstances until the only solution is personnel changes. We prefer to get the real issues up front so the reluctant participants can air their reasons for nonacceptance. Nearly every time we insist on this approach, we find a reasonable solution that makes the reluctant individual an active participant. When all of the key participants are mentally synchronized with the process intentions, the chances for success climb dramatically.

Improvement Efforts Proceed Most Smoothly When There Is Organizational Stability; They Proceed with Inconsistency in the Presence of Instability

If organizational changes are necessary, they should be completed before an improvement effort is initiated. The idea that necessary changes can be made as the improvement process moves forward is flawed. When technical and personnel changes are introduced, attention to implementation is diluted, and results suffer. People are simply too concerned about the changes—and potential effects on the organization—to keep their focus on the improvement process. Our experience shows that periods of backsliding follow most organizational changes.

No business unit is so solid in terms of performance that it will never face the possibility of change. Changes occur due to retirements, voluntary resignations, illness, and so forth. These alterations have to be accepted as part of business life. The organizational changes we refer to are the planned changes due to reorganization, performance necessities, downsizing, and head-count reductions. These changes will negatively affect an improvement effort and are best handled before the process is initiated.

In simple terms, continuous improvement requires a stable environment in which members of the organization at all levels understand the necessity for change and execute against established targets in a concerted manner. Leaders and followers have to be of a single mind as the implementation proceeds.

Partnering to Eradicate Tubular Mentality

Some business organizations are able to generate a high level of cooperation between departments and similar operating units. In a few cases, it seems to occur naturally, as those who lead the groups and those within the groups cooperate as a normal course of business. In other cases, the units recruit the right combination of personalities that results in unforced teamwork. Other groups develop the mutual trust necessary for cross-functional cooperation through years spent working together and providing mutual help in times of need.

In Alice Harper's unit, such positive ingredients are not present; they have to be built. Since we have a deep conviction that people can rise to the necessities of a situation if given sound advice, we would propose elements of partnering to Alice's managers to overcome the lack of unity. To eliminate the silo thinking, we would start by developing a necessary alliance between two traditional adversaries—sales and production.

It is best to start by linking both departments in an effort to jointly determine what factors are truly important to *customers*. Members of the Production Department—including operators, delivery personnel, and managers should be taken with sales representatives to visit key accounts. The purpose is not to meet with buyers or high-level administrators. Rather, this team goes to the factory floor or to the department requiring the provided services. Once in the appropriate location, they visit with the customer's people to discuss what can be done to increase the level of satisfaction. Solutions need not be formulated at this point. It is sufficient to generate a meaningful list of potential improvements that will enhance performance in the customer's eyes. The production personnel return with a firsthand appreciation of what happens to their products and services and how they can become a direct link in improving customer satisfaction. The sales people return with the understanding that they have discovered a valuable, but generally unused resource—as a new ally: the people in production.

Line employees typically come back from such visits enthused over being treated like sensible human beings and prepared to discuss their findings and recommendations with supervisors and managers. Sales representatives and the members from production sit down to jointly develop an action plan for meeting and exceeding the customer needs. That means they use the improvement tools previously suggested, carefully choosing the ones that match the requirements of the solutions. If incoming quality must be improved, for example, so the customer can eliminate inspection, then the joint team can use statistical methods to establish the internal criteria that will ensure that the products and services are "right" before being delivered. What they have now to help them is a plain definition from the customer of the correct specification or how that spec can be improved.

When this internal work is complete, the new sales-production alliance returns to the customer, ready to discuss how they will mutually satisfy and exceed the defined needs. As this discussion unfolds, it becomes abundantly clear to the sales and production representatives that a definite commitment is being made to the customer that requires both sales and production to act in a *partnering* manner. Anything less will jeopardize the commitments being made.

Alice's Sales Manager would realize that production has been linked to customer specifications in such a way that she cannot avoid responsibility for follow-through. From the Production Manager's perspective, an opportunity now exists to bring up matters requiring changes to sales procedure. A list of changes—in such areas as forecasting, order entry, scheduling, and delivery—that would help the manufacturing process can be introduced. Since Alice has already found fault with order entry in sales, we will use that area to illustrate this point.

At one location where we found sales and production deeply antagonistic, order entry proved an excellent area in which to begin forging a much-needed internal alliance. At this site, a two-dollar bill was offered to any employee who could identify a specifications error on sales orders. The time frame was sixty days, and the requirement was to present a copy of the flawed order with a circle around the bad entry. This "experiment" showed that 50 percent of the orders contained at least one error. Production was maintained only because factory workers knew what was really required. After many two-dollar bills were distributed, the sales force had to admit that they needed to link themselves into a better system of getting the right data from the customer to the factory. This was initially resisted by some sales representatives, but eventually the department pledged to meet 100 percent accuracy (which was accomplished in another sixty days).

For Alice, we would next promote partnering in the support functions. Accounting should be advised of the results from the customer visit and of the need for proactive measurements to ensure that customer requirements are met. The Accounting Manager should participate, with members of the accounting and information systems group, in sessions to develop the benchmarks for higher performance.

The human resources group is brought into the alliance by analyzing the customer requirements and the targeted improvements to determine how recruiting, reward systems, compensatory tie-ins, and training can assist the process. One particular service that can be performed by this group is to work closely with the rank-and-file employees—those who create and provide the necessary products and services—to develop their own revised operating procedures. With a clear definition of what the customer wants, the human resources group can be invaluable in helping the sales-production-finance alliance redesign the system by which the customer is satisfied. Engineering can also be brought in at this point to help change procedures and methods to be more efficient and effective. At all times, the directive is simple: any redesigning must relate directly to what the people doing the work indicate will truly enhance their performance. That means nothing is changed unless the workers agree. Trials of suggested changes to verify their efficacy are perfectly legitimate. But as we have mentioned repeatedly, only when those doing the work "own" the process will results be positive and sustained.

Where multiple units of a similar nature exist within the same firm, we have had success using a very simple technique to build cross-unit alliances. To present this technique, it is necessary to consider the potential residing in any and all of the similar units. For purposes of illustration, consider three plants within the same organization, each producing three similar products. Figure 6.1 depicts such a situation, with the additional information that the cost of manufacturing these products varies from low to medium to high. For a service environment, consider that three similar services are being per-

Figure 6.1. Tubular Mentalities Hurt the Firm.

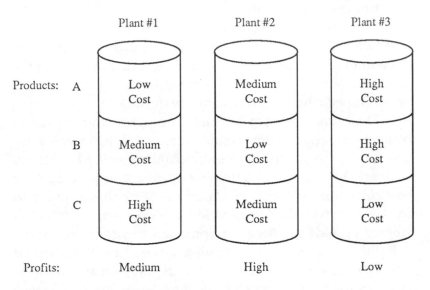

formed at three similar branches or facilities. A hospital, for example, could have services duplicated by two sister locations, with probable variations in how well these services are provided.

If we assume similar selling prices, since plant #2 has only low-to-medium costs, it will have the highest profits. Conversely, since plant #3 has high production costs on two of the three product lines, we can assume low profits. The obvious point is that if the three plants cooperated to find the lowest costs for all products, profits would maximize, and long-term competitiveness would be enhanced. In the service analogy, if the hospitals worked synergistically to have the highest service capability at each site, customer satisfaction and profits would rise accordingly. As simplistic as the example may be, it illustrates the importance of cooperation. In a real-life situation, what are the chances the three plant managers or hospital directors would share information or expertise on their own?

This question can be asked of technical expertise within

line and support groups, of research and engineering departments, about selling skills between product lines or different factories, about development ability, and so forth. Using illustrations similar to Figure 6.1, we have been able to get plant and department managers to form cross-unit or intradepartmental teams focused on finding the best practices. The simplicity of the diagram and the argument does not negate the fact that supposedly world-class companies, with internationally recognizable names, never achieve the full potential of their total resources.

The Heart of Nonimplementation

At this point we return to the critical role key managers play in the successful implementation of a change process. The number one reason for failure, even of a well-intentioned start, is the nonacceptance of the tenets of the change process by these managers, in spite of their positive, cosmetic endorsement.

When the internal assessment is complete and new alliances have provided valuable information on how to satisfy customer needs, key managers have solid information on the readiness of the unit to provide quality, service, accuracy, productivity, delivery, and so forth. If a machine needs repair or should be replaced, professional advice is available on what to do. If a system or procedure interferes with the ability to meet new, higher standards of performance, the cause can now be identified and remedial recommendations proposed. If certain personnel are weak performers or do not provide customer satisfaction, appropriate changes are under consideration. Now comes the critical task of deciding how to modify current behavior to achieve the level of improvements necessary.

As change begins, we find that a strange phenomenon occurs. Managers sense the process will move forward, with or without their support. They become torn as to how they should express themselves. Some openly object, on grounds that the changes are unnecessary or conflict with progress already made. Another group will reluctantly accede, without any real intention of cooperating. Still others will cooperate simply because they accept all directional change as inevitable and beyond question. The majority will give tacit agreement in good faith, while they wait to understand exactly what commitment they are making.

Alice's Sales Manager wanted to be viewed as cooperative. She gave her endorsement and participated enthusiastically in the early stages of the change process. When the time came to make unpleasant decisions—those that would foster the intent of the new process—this manager became a reluctant participant. In spite of her assurances of support, the Sales Manager refused to make internal changes to the sales function.

This type of reaction occurs all too often as the improvement process starts to backslide from the original progress. Key middle managers will strongly endorse a change process without realizing the depth of the commitment they are making. When a "moment of crisis" or crossroads arises, when they have to make a decision that either propels the process forward or sends it backward, they cannot be counted on to continue their strong endorsement. An example that occurs frequently is the following: a key manager has promised to steadfastly support a quality improvement process. A moment of crisis arises when a major order has been rejected and the manager has to accept the return of the delivered goods and incur the expense of the replacement shipment. If that manager backslides by convincing the customer to use part or all of the off-quality product in exchange for a credit to price, the improvement process will begin to deteriorate. A similar example is a hospital administrator who fails to deal with a surgeon whose procedures have become haphazard.

Alice can try to get her key managers to willingly support the change process, but in her position she must be prepared for more political endorsement than real commitment. She could use a professional to talk with her managers to assess the real degree of their willingness to support the new effort; a skilled third party can usually draw out the real inhibitors that could prevent successful implementation by pointing out the internal problems and, more positively, pointing to methods that will enhance improvement.

When Xerox first went looking for the means to overtake its competitors, it likened the necessary inquiries to finding the "warts" in the organization. That analogy is significant because what is needed is a frank analysis of the human ailments that prevent the cooperation necessary across the organization to gain an advantage over firms characterized by greater teamwork. The warts have to be exposed and removed.

The heart of nonimplementation is the key personnel who can dramatically affect those whose actions are necessary for successful implementation. In any business organization there will be an army of people waiting for action signals, both formal and informal, from their leaders. If those leaders act with determination and clear direction, they achieve the kind of followership that makes implementation happen. If the leaders are not truly dedicated, the followers quickly sense that what is wanted is some form of cosmetic action. In this manner, the warts are covered over instead of removed, and progress is temporary.

The heart can be fickle and difficult to understand. What we do know is that genuine progress starts when the attitude to cooperate and succeed moves from the head to the heart: when key people, particularly the middle managers of the organization, set aside their standard operational techniques and honestly try to function in a team environment to make the logic of the improvement process succeed with their people.

To help the reader distinguish between real, heartfelt dedication and the easily given cosmetic endorsement, we offer a simple analogy that we have found useful.

An Axiom: Turkeys, Hawks, and Eagles

For those who go in search of significant improvement, a crucial question is: what *is* the current situation? That query is followed by: what type of actions are we ready to take? We propose an axiom to help explain the circumstances that will be encountered as these questions are answered. It draws an analogy between the animal kingdom, degrees of performance in business, and the reactions that can be expected as improvement efforts are instigated:

> It is easier to work with a turkey than a hawk;
> it is most difficult to work with an eagle.

Turkeys

The term *turkey* has come to refer to a business unit that is in deep financial trouble or an organization that is performing so poorly that it is considered a near hopeless situation—a classic "spin-off," "shut-down," or "rationalization" candidate. While few business units will admit to this designation, they do exist within major corporations, and their presence is generally well known. Our axiom implies that when working with turkeys, any suggestion or command that looks like it will help is readily accepted. These units are eager for change. Improvement can be implemented without the burden of excessive defensiveness on the part of existing personnel. Little downward participation in the decision process is expected, and the unit is usually looking for someone to initiate the required turnaround procedures.

The tendency is to rush into such units, apply the strong, authoritative approach that is expected, and ignore the people factor. Turkeys also require analysis to determine how ready each part is for the necessary alterations. Acceptance of change, even in a seemingly lost situation, represents compromise on the part of the individuals within the unit. No matter how necessary the new procedures may be, old ways must be cast off in favor of new ways. If there is to be positive improvement, some form of negotiating is required before employees willingly begin to implement the altered procedures.

This negotiation can be largely one-directional and highly authoritative, but it need not be. When approaching a bargaining unit, for example, the temptation is to make demands for concessions assuming that everyone accepts the precarious nature of the organization's existence. Alternatively, a frank and honest evaluation of the circumstances might obviate the need for what could easily be interpreted as threatening overtures. Call it benevolent autocracy. The improvement of the turkey begins with the explanation that the unit must create and sustain better performance, that changes to personnel and procedures will be necessary, and that a specific plan to guide those changes will be implemented. The authority of the architect of the plan will be presumed by the participants. What will be expected in return for cooperation will be an understanding of what will happen to those participants and a way to participate in the changes without losing all sense of dignity.

Hawks

In contrast to the obvious poor performer is the less obvious, mediocre-to-good performer. Within large business organizations, there will be units that are not in the close-to-terminal stage but are far from achieving the optimum return on invested resources. These units can actually be making a profit, but the profit is a quarter to a half of what it could be. These units are like hawks: they are flying higher than the turkeys but are not soaring with the eagles.

The readiness for change is considerably less for hawks than for turkeys. Hawks include business units in the comfortable state where a high selling price or a loyal customer base is covering areas of ineffectiveness. Excess costs, high waste, poor quality, spiraling overhead, and poor efficiencies have been rolled into the selling price, concealing the seriousness of these excesses. It is more difficult to convince this group that improvement is necessary.

Within the hawks are managers who at the first mention of potential improvement will become extremely defensive. Consider a manager who has been performing satisfactorily—by personal perception and, in all likelihood, by the existing evaluation and reward systems. When that manager is challenged to do better, his or her agreement is tantamount to admitting that a less-than-optimum performance has been given in the past, and such admission contradicts the manager's self-image of accomplishment. Negativism should be the expected reaction. Anything else should be suspected as bordering on dishonesty.

Hawks can be convinced to rise to higher levels of performance, but two factors will tend to slow the progress:

1.   Hawks will be accustomed to providing relatively conservative improvements. Earnings may rise 5 to 10 percent annually and be linked primarily to capital projects. Movement to a 25 to 50 percent higher level will seem preposterous. The necessary quantum leap to near optimum performance will require arduous convincing or a large measure of direct authority before it will happen.
2.   Improvement techniques will have to be introduced using the current managerial staff. Unless senior management is prepared to make wholesale changes in the staffing or to run the unit entirely by edict, it must be accepted that change will come through present personnel. Those people are accustomed to the gradual improvement characteristic of hawks. A faster pace will require the explanation of the real performance gap, supported by substantial documentation, and an understanding of the logic of the improvement technique.

Hawks are the most pleasant to work with because once they sense the value of what can happen through the improvement process, they also sense the respect that can accrue. Their feeling of pride then becomes a strong motivator. Turning around a turkey is one matter. Taking a good unit to heights never before attained instills an infectious sense of great accomplishment in the participants.

Eagles

At the upper limit of our scale are the *eagles*—organizations that have established market advantages, usually matched by significantly higher-than-normal earnings. This group is generally the least ready for change. Typical eagles include:

- Companies that have a particularly dominant market position supplemented with above-average earnings
- Internal units that generate substantially higher-than-average corporate earnings
- Internal units that generate a disproportionately high percentage of corporate profits
- Recognized leaders in the market by virtue of demonstrably superior quality and performance

Generalizations regarding this group are difficult because eagles tend to split into two categories: those that wish to continue to be leaders and those that want to bask in current accomplishments. In the former category are eagles that constantly seek new challenges and will try virtually any new idea that holds the promise of further improvement. These organizations are aware that many lesser groups are trying to overtake them, and they will do everything possible to maintain their advantage. Change can be fostered for these units. They require only to see how the new initiative fits their existing mode of continuing improvement.

In the latter group are units that are indifferent to the challenge of other organizations. They fancy themselves impervious to a loss of position to a competitor. Their enemy is their own arrogance. These eagles prove to be extremely difficult when a change to procedure must be considered. These units are high achieving and can be expected to hold a sacred position within the larger organization; they believe that a "hands-off" policy applies to them. It is to the second group of eagles-in-danger-of-destruction that the axiom refers.

The managers of such units accept new ideas or innovations only as these concepts can be modified and integrated into the existing self-sufficient cultural attitude. Change is acceptable only as an extension of current management and operating philosophies. Most distasteful to these eagles is any concept that contradicts the perception of perfection that permeates current organizational thinking. To suggest that even greater savings or higher performance is possible through a shift in structure, cutting of overhead costs, setting of new quality standards, revision of systems and procedures, or redeploying of assets is to consider tinkering with perfection. New ideas have to originate within the unit or be strongly modified by local personnel to be palatable to the unit managers. The concept that the idea was "not invented here so it can't be very good" is a real obstacle to progress. A special approach, using senior executive direction, is required to secure implementation of new strategies with the endangered eagles.

This analogy may seem fanciful for the business manager frustrated by nonperformance, but it has been very helpful to us as we have worked to draw out reasons for lack of results. Invariably, as we talk about which category best fits a group, we are able to start isolating the local, cultural factors that are preventing either acceptance or implementation of the guiding concepts. What we seek are the well-camouflaged inner feelings that make key managers pretend to execute rather than sincerely embrace the team role they must play to help make the effort a success. Our animal analogy often helps set the stage for getting at those inner emotions.

Action Study: Levi Strauss and Company

We have stressed the critical need to make a thorough internal assessment before embarking on a major improvement process. We have also argued that attempting to bring continuous improvement to an organization before internal cooperation is at high levels dooms the effort. A business unit that wants to achieve and sustain world-class status must not have silos around departments or plants, must utilize all internal strengths, and must seek constant improvement. A logical question in response to this statement is: if an organization already has world-class status in many areas, do the same rules apply? Our action study was written by William C. McAdory, formerly the manager of quality improvement for Levi Strauss and Company, one of the leading apparel manufacturers in the world. We let him relate what can happen when a high-performing organization goes in search of improvement.

After struggling through the early implementation phases of our Total Quality effort, there are two things I am sure of: It isn't free, and it ain't easy!

For those of us who have been the quality professionals in our organizations, I'm quite sure we can share many stories of the pain and suffering it took to get the efforts launched. In fact, not long into the effort I was not at all sure that I had not made a serious career mistake.

As the organization struggled with the quality process, it became painfully clear that I was expected to have the workable ideas and plans to overcome the frequent sticking points. It became clear to me over time that there were some things missing from the how-to books. These turned out not to be implementation issues but steps I believe must be taken prior to implementation.

Our pursuit of a Total Quality Improvement effort taught me many lessons about implementing TQI and about the company. In preparing this article I chose three of those lessons that if known at the beginning would have made a real difference in our progress to date.

I present them in the order in which I believe they should be addressed by an organization starting a quality journey. The first suggestion is: align the organizational development/human resources (OD/HR) function with the quality process very early. The quality effort as a corporate strategy requires its inclusion in the mission of the OD/HR functions. Once aligned, the OD/HR resources can help with the second lesson: perform an organizational assessment. Simply put, how ready is the organization for the change that is about to take place? What is the nature of the corporate culture? The final lesson is: take the time to research the various approaches to Total Quality and tailor an approach that fits your company.

Aligning OD/HR with Quality

The quality process at Levi Strauss and Company was originally sponsored by a divisional president. That meant that other key executives in the company were not sponsors. This resulted in the OD/HR functions getting their mission and objectives from an executive who was not involved with the quality process. However, we assumed that OD/HR would be there and support the new effort when needed. Correct? Not quite. They tried, but those folks have their plates full most of the time, their resources fully committed, and they don't have people standing around waiting for an assignment. Furthermore, their mission and objectives were being set from a different frame of reference. What resulted were "conflicting priorities," as they were not being measured on the success of the quality program.

As a result of the conflicting priorities, the Director of Quality Enhancement created a separate support staff to deliver the necessary training and consultation to implement the quality process. This resulted in two departments within the company delivering the same type of services. Confusing? You bet. If you want this, call OD; if you want that, call Quality. It wasn't long before the OD and Quality folks were getting together, scratching their heads wondering what was going on themselves. The time spent collaborating on the planning and decision making was wasteful, and the ownership dynamics made this basically unworkable. To manage the organizational transition to Total Quality, the synergy had to be created between the OD and the Quality functions.

Organizational Assessment

The organizational assessment takes a look at the organization from two perspectives. First, a look back as to what kind of initiatives had been launched in the past. Of those, which were successful and which were not, and why? Second, the assessment takes a close look at the current state of the organization. Is business up or down? Are managers pressed for time and harried beyond reason? Is there a general reason for undertaking a change?

Had we done a proper assessment, we would have found some interesting aspects of the company that could—and should—have been taken into account when the implementation of the quality process was planned. A critical aspect was that the company had been undergoing a series of organizational changes that were shrinking as well as flattening the company, even though the company was very prosperous. This resulted in real fears of personal security, as well as reallocation of work. People were generally on an emotional low, with a higher workload. An assessment of the Levi Strauss and Company culture would have revealed some characteristics that could be leveraged to facilitate the change and some that would have to be overcome to maximize success.

Even though the company's recent shrinking and flattening created general feelings of insecurity, there were pockets of complacency. The company is noted for its family image, which creates a paternalistic atmosphere of protecting the employees. The feeling was one of "no matter what happens, the company will take care of me." In other words, "the company is making money, what is the crisis? Why this big quality push?" There was a real resistance to change. Another aspect of our "paternalistic" atmosphere was that there is a balance between concern for the people and the need to accomplish tasks. This required that the quality approach strike a good balance between these two elements.

Goals were generally set at the top, with minimal feedback. Further, there was limited delegation of decisions. This resulted in a malaise, with people waiting on "management" to lead the charge. This spelled real problems for our empowered, participative approach to improvement.

What we were faced with was a passive resistance characterized by no one objecting to the quality process, but also no one doing anything. People were trained, quality policies issued, and meetings held. But there was no identification of major business projects/issues to rally around. The whole thing kind of meandered along. Some time into the effort, there developed a covert resistance. No one was publicly criticizing the process; however, numerous barriers began to pop up. The most popular one was that the "process" was too bureaucratic. Bureaucracy is bad, therefore the "process" was defective.

Lastly, but of major significance, was the lack of teamwork in the company—especially across departments.

The cornerstone of our approach to TQI was to build on the team approach with its obvious benefits. However, we were confronted with major dysfunctions as the teams were brought together. This was manifested by people protecting their position and function rather than focusing on the effectiveness of business process.

Choosing the Right Approach

One thing is clear to me today, and that is that there is no one way to implement Total Quality. In fact, there is probably not a "one way" approach within any company. We could have spent six months or more traveling the country looking at how other companies were approaching quality. We needed to examine the successes and try to determine why they were successful and if any of the good characteristics were present at Levi Strauss.

What did we learn? There is a lot to be said about a "project breakthrough" to get a skeptical group on board. The longer-term strategic planning approach, however worthy, only works in the appropriate environment. Our people wanted results and wanted them rather quickly. There was a clear understanding for the need for planning, but as discussed above, there needed to be early proof that this whole thing worked. Further, the entrepreneurial nature of many of our managers led them to reject a centralized plan for Total Quality. Creating a customized approach for the individual business units based on a successful project as a benchmark is clear to me today as the better approach for Levi Strauss and Company.

We're Making Progress

We have learned a lot from the initial struggle to launch our process and are incorporating these and other learnings as we move into the 90s. We are much like others attempting to create an environment of continuous improvement. We are currently revisioning our approach in the third year. Have we failed in our effort? Hardly! The quality process in some parts of our organization is very nearly institutionalized. There is a commonality of language that pervades the organization. In virtually every meeting, I hear people discussing "customers," "suppliers," and "requirements." Cross-functional teams are popping up all over, covering a whole range of issues. And sound, clear measures of key business processes are hanging outside the doors of key managers' offices.

Summary

In this chapter, we presented ways to deal with the obstacles to a continuous improvement effort. We discussed eradicating tubular mentality through business partnering alliances and listed four characteristics that we have found to accompany successful implementation efforts. Obstacles to implementing a continuous improvement effort are not insurmountable, but it is critical to be aware of the number one reason for failure: nonacceptance of the change process by key managers and their often nonverbalized resistance. Managers must be willing to set aside normal operating procedures and honestly try to function in a team environment. We presented an analogy to the animal kingdom as a way to help readers assess any local, cultural factors that may impede improvement efforts. Real progress begins with the formation of alliances and moves steadily forward as silos are torn down.

Chapter Seven

◆

INTERNAL
BUSINESS PARTNERING

To successfully execute a continuous improvement effort, an organization selects an improvement logic and conducts an assessment of its internal culture to determine the state of readiness to implement that logic. Most firms discover from their assessments that significant changes in traditional thinking are required before readiness is at sufficient levels to ensure the success of the program. There are many reasons for this lack of readiness, but generally none more prevalent—or crucial—than the lack of full support from the collective human resources of the organization—what we call the various constituencies. Parts will be ready to execute, but because of existing paradigms that inhibit true acceptance of the improvement logic, the totality of the organization will not be fully prepared to implement.

Through our near-to-life anecdote we have attempted to illustrate how various key managers are often particularly difficult converts to the improvement logic. They will overtly acknowledge the value of the concepts but secretly harbor misgivings about possible negative personal impacts. These managers will cosmetically endorse the process and actively participate in planning sessions. They will withhold committed involvement, however, when faced with decisions that require putting aside their traditional viewpoints and acting in a team manner. They will especially demonstrate nonsupport when changes are required inside their areas of control.

154

Alice Harper and her key managers struggled for over three years to develop an improvement process that would create a competitive advantage for them. After three years, they are doing little more than treading water. Alice has learned, at least, that there is no easy solution to her dilemma and that the real enemy is hidden in the hearts of her various constituencies. She now knows she has to somehow get those groups and their leaders to accept the logic of the improvement effort and to change their behavior accordingly. She knows she must forge alliances so that her unit can move forward toward the elusive advantage they all seek.

Alice decided, as much from despair as from determination, to assemble her key managers one more time and attempt to sell them on the benefits of the improvement logic.

Alice Forges Her Alliances

It was customary during the year-end holiday season for Alice Harper to host a luncheon for her direct reports. At this year's event, she determined it would be appropriate to toast the coming season and also to discuss what had crystallized for her as the major impediment to successful implementation of the improvement process.

Following a toast in which she wished the best of the season and the coming year to her associates, Alice remained standing and looked thoughtfully at her audience. Several individuals became a bit nervous, but all waited patiently for her next comments.

"You know," she began slowly, "it's traditional at this time to reflect on the year that we've had as a group. This year, I'm not going to do that. We made some money. We kept our jobs. But we did not achieve our full potential. Let it go at that. What I want to reflect on is three years of trying to pull this group together as a team. That we have not done, and that—I believe—is why we have results that do not reflect anything close to our full potential."

The group settled a little deeper into their chairs and increased their concentration on the boss.

Alice moved slowly around the table as she continued. Pausing behind the Production Manager, she said "We make a good product. That keeps us in business. We have loyal customers who want that product and are used to getting it from us." She moved toward the Sales Manager. "We have a sales force that has good relationships with those customers, supported by a customer service group that works very hard to keep the relationships at a high level of satisfaction." There were a few nods to this comment.

"We have an accounting group," she continued, "that spends long, hard hours making sense of what we do and trying to help us improve our performance. And we have a quality group that constantly implores us to be better at all we do. The purchasing group has worked hard to get help from our suppliers."

Alice paused next to the Quality Control Manager and looked at everyone around the table. "There is just one thing wrong, as I see it," she remarked. "We are all doing what we do for ourselves—and not for each other. We are not a team. We are a collection of fairly good managers as individuals. We are not a cohesive unit working with each other."

Alice received no comment. She expected none. As she continued to move slowly around her audience, she said in a very serious manner, "Since this is the time when people traditionally make vows, I'm going to make one . . . and I'll ask each of you to do the same." After receiving a few unsolicited nods of agreement, Alice said, "Next year, I vow to treat all the people working for me as though they were partners with me in a private business."

From the nonresponse she received, Alice knew elaboration was in order. "What I mean," she added, "is that I want us to conduct our business as though we had made a leveraged buyout. If we had, we would all be principal owners of the business, heavily in debt to repay the loan we took out, and looking for increased profits to secure our fortunes. In that sense, we would all be partners and would treat each other as though our mutual success—or failure—was at stake."

"You mean if we do things to hurt another group, we end up hurting ourselves," the Accounting Manager attempted to help.

"That's right," Alice agreed. "If this was our business and our personal fortunes depended on the success of that business, I think we would start working together more closely. We would also do everything we could to get the full cooperation of our workers and our suppliers. That is what I want us to do next year. I want us to act like our future depends on treating each other as well as we think we treat our customers."

"And our suppliers," the Senior Buyer added.

"That's correct," said Alice. "We have a network that includes our suppliers, the various parts of this business unit, and our customers. Starting January 2, I want us to function as though satisfying the needs of everyone within that network was our aim. The way to do that I believe, is to look at people within the network as though they were our partners. It's a mental game, but I want you to approach the constituents of the network as though they were co-owners with you."

"That's a lot of people," the Sales Manager enjoined. "Do you think we can please that many individuals?"

"Probably not," was Alice's reply. "What we can do is get out of our usual paradigms and start thinking more like a team, rather than as individuals. I'm very serious about this, and I will measure performance next year against what I see as progress in this area."

"You mean you will measure how we perform," the Production Manager questioned, "in terms of what we do for each other? How about how many units we produce and ship? How about how much money we make?"

"I'm convinced the profits will be there if we can improve as partners," Alice replied. "Look, we have all the tools. We've had all the training we need. What we don't have is results. Each time I talk with you as a group or as individuals, I find a strong endorsement for improving what we do. I also find you want the other person to change. You want the other groups to improve performance so your lives will be easier. That doesn't work. It hasn't worked. Starting next year, we are going to function as though what we do together, as a unit, is what *counts. I want us to start thinking as partners, not as individuals. We're smart enough to do that."*

Alice's comments were followed by a discussion that lasted over an hour. Early questions sought clarification, but as the conversation continued, it became clear to everyone that Alice was going to make a final attempt to make continuous improvement happen through an alliance of her managers. This time she was going to get everyone to approach the way they did business as though their future depended on high levels of mutual cooperation. This time she was going to forge alliances within her organization that would lead to constituencies applying good techniques together, not in isolation. She was determined to try what we call business partnering.

Business Partnering: Employee Involvement

In Chapter Three, we defined business partnering as "the creation of cooperative business alliances between constituencies within an organization and between an organization and its suppliers and customers." Business partnering is a process through which individuals in all parts of an organization—working together and with suppliers and customers—improve the relationships and performances that make a business work and survive. In this chapter, following our edict to begin within an organization, we examine internal business partnering.

Up to this point, we have argued the following: an improvement process must begin with an internal assessment to answer the following questions.

1. Where is the unit currently, both in comparison to its competition and in the eyes of its customers?
2. Where does the unit have to be in order to survive and stay ahead of its competition?
3. Where do its leaders and customers want to be in the future?

As managers develop the answers to these questions, they become aware of the obstacles—both of a cultural and an operational nature—that may impede the improvement effort. We have discussed benchmarking and improvement tools to create an operating strategy and have warned against the critical problem posed by nonacceptance of (and resistance to) change by key managers. We have discussed ways to deal with this problem.

Without the sincere support and clear understanding of all constituencies in an organization—including managers and employees—an improvement effort will fail. A dynamic leader can attempt to force needed improvements by replacing all reluctant managers. If this happens, progress comes more as a result of the new managers driving their people to try proven techniques than from any modifications resulting from the improvement logic. Partnering doesn't occur because there is no real sharing of resources, dedication to mutually beneficial objectives, or recognition for a strong group effect.

The type of partnering we propose here is called employee involvement (EI). EI has been discussed in the business literature for many years. It is recognized as a central feature of the modern approach to business improvement. As usual, the logic is real; the positive results are elusive. In the United States, we simply do not have the same record of utilizing our human talent as do some of our more formidable and successful foreign competitors, particularly the Japanese. Newt Hardie (1990), vice-president of quality for Milliken and Company, states the problem succinctly when he says, "We use only 10 percent of the capability of our workers." These are strong words, coming from one of the U.S. business organizations with the best EI records. What an enormous potential must be residing within the minds and hearts of American workers! Leaders must tap that reserve to gain a stronger global position for our businesses. Our successes have been confined to distinct islands of progress, instead of being a nationwide characteristic. The missing ingredient is utilization of the total, national talent pool.

Before developing our argument on utilizing EI as a strong element of business partnering, we present another near-to-life story that illustrates what can happen when willing resources are not tapped. We invite the reader to join Alice Harper in another meeting at her plant site, where a serious competitive disadvantage is being attacked—for about the tenth time.

Alice and Stanley

The meeting was moving slowly. John Attwood, who had agreed to facilitate this action team, had explained all the ground rules and had clarified role issues for participants: everyone was to participate, be honest, not attack others, and deal with issues, not people. Now he was patiently waiting for the discussion to lead to some possible solutions to the problem. This particular action team had been asked to work on the problem of why the rolling metal mill was unable to control the caliper (thickness) of the finished sheet. This sheet was wound into large reels that were taken to forming presses, where the finished products were stamped out. The products were then sold with the guarantee of caliper stability within an industry-accepted range. For most products, the range was easily met, but in a profitable thin grade line, the mill was unable to hold tolerance and was encountering a reject rate approaching 25 percent. Everyone had been living with this problem for fifteen years, but a recent emphasis on quality by two major customers was causing those companies to return all product made from reels that did not fall within the acceptable range. Rejected material had accumulated to the point where it was consuming all allocated space in the warehouse. The mill manager had organized an action team to resolve how the reels could be made within the required range. The alternative was to quit making that grade until a solution was reached.

After a bit of prodding, Attwood was able to generate a few suggestions and a reasonable amount of discussion. Nothing really struck him as a potential solution, however, and he continued to prod the group for more ideas. Eventually, he decided to call on Stanley Kapchak. Stanley was a thirty-year veteran of the maintenance force. He was a member of the action team because he was considered one of the best mechanics in the mill. Attwood discovered he was a reluctant participant.

"Stanley," Attwood finally asked, in an attempt to draw the mechanic into the converstaion, "you've been around the mill for a long time. What are your thoughts?"

"On what?" was his abrupt response.

"On the question of why we can't hold caliper on the lower-gauge sheet?" was Attwood's patient reply.

"I think it's in the valving," was Kapchak's short reply.

"Now goddamn it, Stan," the mill superintendent cried out. "You've been saying that, and you're wrong. The valving is totally unrelated to sheet caliper. Those are two separate issues."

Kapchak slid slowly down in this chair and folded his arms resolutely over his chest.

"Hold on a minute," Alice Harper interjected, noticing the scowl that was spreading across Stanley's face. "I would like to hear what Stanley has to say. Come on, Stan. Tell us about the valving."

Kapchak stirred uncertainly in his chair and did not respond. Alice decided to persevere. She moved slowly toward the reluctant mechanic and stopped when she was directly in line between Kapchak and the mill superintendent. With Alice in that position, neither individual could see the other because she blocked their line of sight.

"Well," Kapchak started slowly. "I remember we put those new valves in fifteen years ago to replace some worn-out units. They were a different size, but the engineers said that was all right. They would work. Well, they ain't worked. Not from the day they was put in. The week after they was started up, we lost caliper, not across all the line, but especially in the thin grades. And we ain't got that caliper back yet."

Patricia Long, the Technical Manager, feverishly waved her hand. "Remember, Stan. We also changed all the piping from those valves at the same time."

"And we put in the new pressing system," said the Quality Control Manager.

"So what?" Kapchak grunted. "It was them valves that started the problem."

Alice stepped toward the chart pad that was in the center of the front part of the room. "Maybe there is a relationship," she encouraged. "Let's draw up the process before and after the changes. Do you think we can remember what happened?"

The next thirty minutes were consumed with reconstructing the fifteen-year-old changes. During that period, Stanley Kapchak became the chief architect of the drawing that was being developed on the chart pad. He also carefully avoided the glares directed at him by the mill superintendent.

When the drawings were finished, Attwood took the group through an analysis of the before-and-after aspects of the changes to the mill process to determine what might have been affected.

Finally, the Quality Control Manager said, "You know, it is definitely possible that we matched the new piping to the old valve size and that it is constricting the hydraulic flow in the thinner ranges."

Several heads nodded agreement.

"Well, how can we find out?" Alice asked.

"We can check the old prints to see," Patricia Long volunteered. "If there is a mismatch, we can change one line to see what happens."

The team quickly agreed to that suggestion, and the meeting was adjourned until an answer was available. Two weeks later, the team met again to accept resolution of the problem. The prints revealed that a mismatch in piping and valving did exist. When the trial change was made, caliper came immediately into the specification range. After Alice thanked the group for their effort, the mill superintendent cornered Stanley Kapchak.

"I want to apologize, Stan," was the sincere remark. "I almost shut you up when you had the right idea all along."

"Had it for fifteen years," was the crisp response.

"Well, why didn't you tell me sooner?" the mill superintendent implored.

"I tried! Couple of times! You wouldn't take the time to listen to me," Stanley said with a broad smile.

Tapping the Human Reservoir

Realizing the full potential of employee participation begins with the CEO, who must take this message throughout the organization, particularly to the sites where products and services are created: EI will be a reality, and the results will not be a short-term success story. The need for everyone's involvement, the desire to develop partnering, and the rewards for participation have to be clearly articulated. A wide range of responses should be expected, from absolutely no reaction to cautious enthusiasm. Patience, support, and perseverance then become the tools to make certain EI becomes a reality.

Preston Trucking, an organization with a history of adversarial relations between management and labor, learned the value of turning around such a situation ("Preston Profits by . . . ," 1990). Using the simple value statement that "Preston People Make the Difference," management began to show a sincere interest in developing EI. Skeptical employees, members of the Teamsters' Union, watched cautiously as Preston leaders became more interested in and responsive to employee input. Within two years of beginning the new approach, the company was benefiting from more than 10,000 employee-volunteered profit improvement ideas. A new feature included keeping the union informed on the firm's financial condition and plans for the future. Such open information sharing would be considered heresy at most U.S. businesses. Preston went further. Union stewards are now invited to attend training sessions with managers to expose the rank-and-file to all features of Preston's operations. We find this situation to be a great example of the type of trade-off that can occur—10,000 potentially profitable ideas for a chance to be treated as sensible, contributing human beings who are part of the Preston partnering network.

The current national labor force has the following characteristics that directly affect workers' willingness to participate:

- Workers must have a reason for what they are asked to do. The era of blind obedience is gone.
- They have to see a mutual benefit, for the company and for themselves.
- They want to know how their work affects the direction in which the company is moving. Since they are key to making the ship go, they prefer to know where it is going so they can contribute to helping it get there.

The process of cultivating workers' input can be called employee involvement, participative management, or employee participation. The labels are unimportant. The idea is to tap the creativity and knowledge of the human resources of an organization. Mutual benefits can include increased profits from lower costs. They should also include making the job of achieving those results less arduous and more satisfying.

Since their work ultimately brings the desired results, workers have a right to know how they affect the chosen course of action and to have some measure of control over what they do or, at least, over how they do it. The final, perhaps most crucial, link occurs when mangement ties worker performance directly to the fortunes of the organization by creating a pool from earnings that can be distributed to those creating the necessary improvements. At that point workers understand their role, contribute ideas for improvement, and share in the positive results. Under these conditions, tapping of the human reservoir becomes a reality, and partnering takes on long-term meaning.

Success using this approach can be found in many interesting places. Wanting to get 36,000 managers and employees at 1,500 branches spread all across Canada focused on customer service, the Royal Bank of Canada decided an employee-oriented effort was necessary. Jack Klassen (1988, p. 3), vice-president of quality of services and productivity, puts the effort into perspective: "We want to be a customer-focused business. We want to unleash the potential of our people. We want to be the best and one of the most profitable financial services in Canada. You start with these strategic objectives . . . that have to be communicated throughout the organization, and translated by local managers so employees know what the objectives mean to them and their jobs—how they can contribute to making it happen."

Klassen explains how this thinking led to what they termed Royal Bank's B-4 initiative: "B-4, which stands for 'Building Business and Battling Bureaucracy,' is not a short-term program. It's a management system, a franchise mentality, a permanent decentralization of authority through clusters of branches, called areas. The idea of B-4 is to decentralize our customer decisions to the closest possible level to the customer. It's empowering our area managers and the people to deal with customer service situations right then and there" (p. 3).

Client surveys were developed and administered one week every quarter in each of the branches. The survey asked customers questions about factors important to customer service in financial institutions: employee appearance, reliability, efficiency, confidence, and caring. The data from the surveys are analyzed and reviewed by the staff at each branch. In this way they gain what Bob Aylward, manager of customer service and operations, says is "a clear understanding of the client's perception of our service" (Klassen, 1988, p. 3). He elaborates on the ensuing actions: "The staff zeros in on the weak or priority areas, and develops a game plan, using a process called Group Action. It's a participative process which helps managers run meetings that get input from employees. The same is true of our local employee survey, which we administer yearly to everyone in our branches. It measures 22 attributes which our staff told us would exist in a work environment where they would feel proud to work."

Employee committees were eventually established to assess progress toward resolving identified client and employee issues. These committees recommend awards that correspond to levels of progress. Aylward comments: "All branch personnel receive customer service training, and some are singled out for recognition. We want to profile those people who go the extra mile for clients, so that kind of behavior becomes the norm rather than the exception. In recent years, we've rediscovered the importance of the client. What we're trying to do is get service to be like religion—something you practice every day."

Royal Bank is obviously trying to get that religion by involving as many of its people as possible in implementing the strategies that are important to the bank's success. Its secret lies in the bank's ability to get willing participation from those constituencies so they will contribute ideas and concepts that make the strategies come to life.

Power of Idea Generation

The concept of idea generation systems has been around for many years. In most instances, management supports the concept for a brief period as they see immediate gains. When the effort requires feedback, patience, support, and accepting small ideas as well as the "big" hits, managers are likely to drop the intensity and put away the suggestion box, much to the chagrin of those employees who genuinely tried to contribute meaningful ideas. In world-class organizations, idea generation may not be called a suggestion system because that format has fallen into disuse, but a modified version of the same concept is being taken to new heights of success by some very dedicated managements. These managements have found that the generation of ideas is an important method of strengthening internal alliances. Tapping the deep reservoir of employee knowledge and creativity has become a daily activity—with astounding results—at Toyota, Nissan, Florida Power and Light, Milliken, Motorola, Texas Instruments, Moore Business Forms, and others.

Whatever label is used, the intention is the same. Management needs to get workers to freely give their ideas, comments, suggestions, and recommendations on how to make their jobs more satisfying and rewarding, while saving the company some dollars in the process. Done properly, work becomes less arduous, the quality of the products and services improves, costs decrease, the management-worker alliance solidifies, and employees gain more control over job performance. It truly can be a win-win situation for all members of the organization.

Ford Motor Company has provided opportunities for workers to make meaningful contributions to improving their working environment (Ephlin, 1990). Many employees at Ford's EI locations report increased satisfaction, fulfillment, and a greater sense of self-worth. The Ford idea was to create a work environment in which employees willingly helped improve the performance of the firm. The rank-and-file could make such contributions by:

- Identifying opportunities for improvement
- Participating in team problem solving
- Analyzing the cause of problems
- Suggesting alternative solutions
- Implementing the best methods

Ford has learned, like most of the successful EI firms, that team problem solving is a keystone of employee participation. Team problem solving starts with exposing volunteers to working in teams and performing basic problem solving. With early successes comes the motivation for more reluctant workers to participate. As the process continues and is rewarded by management, a few firms have found that EI moves to a higher level: employees recommend the areas of investigation and freely form teams to seek ways not just to solve problems but to capitalize on opportunities. The same techniques are applied, but the teams now focus on improvements that do not derive from inherent difficulties.

The "Motorola Family" has taken that organization to a

higher level of idea generation where workers need little or no management encouragement to suggest improvements. With over 100,000 employees, Motorola assumes that if management creates the correct environment, workers will continuously recommend ways to improve job performance (Hooker, 1991). By inviting (and requiring) EI in running its business, Motorola receives thousands of new ideas each month. Motorola's version of participative management has withstood the usual lack of management endurance and remained in place for ten years.

The published purpose of the Motorola process is succinct: "to continually assess the process of performing work and to change it in ways which will reduce defects and reduce cycle time" (Hooker, 1991). Motorola clearly stated the objectives of its form of EI and idea generation. In 1987, the corporation stated its overall goal as achieving a 10X quality improvement by 1989, 100X by 1991, and to be at the Six Sigma level throughout the firm by 1992. This level means that defects— defined as anything that causes customer dissatisfaction—will be less than .0003 percent. To date, Motorola is satisfied the timetable is being met.

For organizations that might be intimidated by the magnitude of the Motorola commitment, there are examples that prove the power of ideas can be tapped in very simple ways. So long as management is willing to approach workers with true respect, sustain their support, and recognize their achievements, the results can be truly astonishing. Richard W. Wratten, president of Transamerica Insurance Group, reports that his organization started an EI process with an "idea generator" in 1986 (1990). Forty-five hundred employees participated as informal groups were organized from *all* departments. These groups were confronted with a simple question: how can we do our work more efficiently? A committee made up of individuals from different functions and different levels of the organization was formed to judge the responses.

Since there is generally a correlation between work simplification and cost savings, a special feature was added to the effort. For each dollar of savings that accrued to the firm, points for obtaining catalogue gifts were given to the "idea generator." The top teams, as selected by the committee, were given a sixty-second "run" through a gift warehouse: the winners and a companion could keep as many items as they could collect in a shopping cart in that time. The average value of these "runs" was $4,500. Wratten reports that $27,000,000 worth of usable ideas were generated, with $20,000,000 appearing on the profit statement within eighteen months. Since jobs were performed better, employee satisfaction rose dramatically, and the company's prosperity was enhanced. Transamerica obviously found EI and idea generation to be a win-win situation.

Organizations that go in search of similar success should be alert to the connection between EI and idea generation. Don Ephlin (1990), retired vice-president of the UAW and now a lecturer at Massachusetts Institute of Technology, gives some sound advice for those who wish to tap the wealth of employee advice. He states, "Employees have to see improvement is in their best interest and not just something to help management." His key to EI is for management to trust the rank-and-file, thereby getting the workers to trust management. His message may seem maudlin, but our experience has schooled us to emphasize the power of trust as a building block to success. The workers we have encountered consistently give greater effort, more willingly, when approached in an honest, sincere manner. It is only when they feel cheated or sense they are being treated in a demeaning manner that they mobilize to withhold productivity.

The best firms trust their workers and have permanent action teams in each department or plant. These teams continuously generate ideas on how to improve anything and everything the firm does. For these organizations, the power of ideas has become a part of the culture and an organized means of sustaining continuous improvement.

Action Study: Milliken & Co., Inc.

None of the preceding concepts work for long unless those who partic-ipate are recognized for their efforts. As contributions are rewarded and individuals and teams are cited for their efforts, enthusiasm grows and the input multiplies. The rewards can be monetary or nonmonetary, but the recognition must be sincere. One of the most successful organiza-tions in that aspect of the partnering effort is the 125-year-old textile manufacturer, Milliken & Co., Inc. This story begins in 1980, when the CEO, Roger Milliken, realized that Japanese competitors had surpassed the U.S. manufacturers of textiles and had done so with older equip-ment. Japanese leadership was resulting in higher quality and produc-tivity and lower delivered costs.

In 1981, Roger Milliken decided to recapture the lead in textile manufacturing by launching a "Pursuit of Excellence." Many firms em-barked on similar crusades at that time, inspired by the Peters and Water-man (1982) book and the growing national awareness of the need for quality improvement. Milliken's effort was destined to be more effec-tive than most, as evidenced by its beginning. The CEO led the senior manager's pledge to three important axioms:

- I will listen.
- I will not shoot messengers.
- I understand that management is the problem. . . . I am the problem.

The organization was flattened, and managers became "process improvers." Employees became "associates," empowered to shut down machines for quality or safety. These associates were trained to under-stand the entire manufacturing process. Monthly surveys were sent out to discover what customers wanted and needed, so the associates could help provide new levels of customer satisfaction. The open-door policy, fostered by some companies, has become for Milliken a "no-door" policy in which the managers have moved out to the common area that as-sociates and leadership now share.

Since the company had identified the three largest barriers to success as (1) top management, (2) middle management, and (3) first-line management, it knew the paradigm switch had to be from an autocratic to a democratic culture. Piecework pay was stopped because it contradicted the quality incentive in favor of volume and favored individual effort over teamwork. Sales commissions for volume were similarly dropped. Milliken essentially built a new model for performance based on people, as opposed to its previous orientation toward technology and new equipment.

Of particular interest at Milliken is its remarkable results with idea generation. Figure 7.1 documents Milliken's progress in terms of ideas/associate/year since 1984. With 13,000 associates, simple multipli-

Figure 7.1. Milliken & Co.: Opportunities for Improvement.

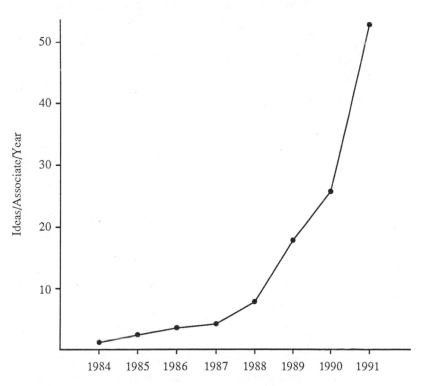

Source: Milliken & Co., Inc. Used by permission.

cation reveals how many "opportunities for improvement" are generated. Response to these ideas comes in two forms. An acknowledgment and thank you is delivered within twenty-four hours, and some form of action is taken within seventy-two hours. Most ideas are about improving customer satisfaction. Thus, the Milliken people can produce cost-savings as well as cost-generating ideas, so long as satisfaction is improved in the eyes of the customer. Teams are often involved in their idea generation systems, and in 1991 there were over 10,000 team projects recorded.

To recognize those teams and their individual associates, Milliken convenes quarterly "Sharing Rallies." At these events, up to 200 people gather for a one-day series of presentations by production, administrative, and management associates. The presentations document the results of ideas generated within the company. The emphasis is placed on sharing good results before an audience of peers and upper management. The subjects covered at the rallies include:

- Corrective action teams
- Success stories
- Recognition stories
- Customer and supplier action teams
- Innovative accomplishments
- Quick picks: small improvements that can lead to a real difference in performance

Each associate in the audience rates the presenters, using a 1–6 scale, on such characteristics as:

- Identification of the problem
- Use of quality improvement process techniques
- Course of corrective action taken
- Evidence of lasting results

As Tom Malone, president of Milliken explains, "The purpose is to create an environment that will allow people to contribute to the maximum of their capability . . . for management to thank them, make them heroes for doing so, and to have some fun in the process." All attendees at the rally are recognized for their participation, with each receiving a certificate signed by Malone and Roger Milliken. "Super sharer" grand prizes are awarded to the winners, who are selected by audience balloting.

Milliken believes recognizing the type of contributions documented at these rallies and honoring the involved associates is important to the success of its improvement process. This sharing of ideas and innovations in such a supportive atmosphere, with the visible presence of the most senior leaders, has to be effective. For Milliken, the power of full participation from its collective human resources has propelled the company back into a leadership position. Today, Milliken ranks as the leading world-class textile manufacturer.

Summary

Nothing encourages employee involvement so much as a true crisis. Most of the success stories of the 1980s reflected a need for rapid improvement in order to survive. Xerox found that a Japanese copier could be purchased for what it cost Xerox to make a similar unit. Harley-Davidson, Milliken, and others found foreign competitors taking traditional American markets offshore with higher quality and lower cost for products made from the same machinery. In these instances, management and workers rallied together to reach new heights of performance to secure survival and profitability.

Companies not functioning in a crisis state can also create and sustain an improvement effort. In this chapter, we have argued that what is required is confidence in the power of the average worker and management to raise performance by magnitudes of 40–100 percent. Also required is a level of trust and honesty on a world-class scale that will induce workers to give freely of their knowledge and skills so higher performance can be achieved. Business partnering begins to emerge when a firm overcomes the traditional misgivings associated with an alliance between parties unaccustomed to working together as closely as is necessary for success in today's world environment.

Managers must look upon their employee pool as an energy source. If the efficiency of that source is 10-20 percent, who should be blamed for the waste? What does it matter? The organization incurs the same cost: a distinctive disadvantage. Blame management or blame labor, the organization will go down with both groups on board. Leadership is the answer, leadership that can harness the full power of the human energy source to an engine that will take everyone to where the unit has to be to survive and sustain a competitive advantage.

The vehicle for this journey is employee involvement. When management is able to focus the intensity of all employees on necessary improvements, the results can be overwhelming. When employees see improvement as being in their best interest as well as the firm's, they can unleash a flow of energy that will carry the organization to levels of performance never before dreamed possible. This energy has to be tapped and channeled into meaningful, long-term alliances, which become the heart of the internal portion of business partnering. These alliances are the catalyst that makes continuous improvement a reality.

Chapter Eight

◆

BUSINESS PARTNERING
WITH SUPPLIERS

As an organization begins to understand and apply the principles of partnering, employees will start to develop the internal alliances necessary to make beneficial improvements. As these alliances start to produce performance levels beyond the more traditional improvement pace, an enthusiasm will be generated. This enthusiasm will be for extending the alliances to other interested organizations. When an organization finds itself in what we have termed Phase 3 (critique and continuance) of improvement evolution, either at particular locations or throughout a division or the entire firm, it can begin to expand the concept of partnering.

Our recommendation is to first extend partnering to suppliers: those organizations that provide the products, materials, machinery, and services needed to make the business process work. We choose involving suppliers first to help enhance the quality and capability of the organization's internal process before moving to customers. Let us check in with Alice Harper once again.

Alice Beyond the Crossroads

It had taken Alice Harper another year, but with the patience of her leaders and her refusal to accept defeat, her plant's objectives had been met and exceeded. Her managers had torn down their silos and made—

and kept—the kind of mutual commitments she had proposed. Alliances had developed within the plant, and workers were generating improvement ideas and helping in the selling process. Alice's partnering efforts had paid off: promises made were promises kept; mutual dependency was the rule, not the exception; performance levels were constantly improving, and the higher results were sustained.

Alice's people were now considering how they might utilize what they had learned from their effort to make even further strides, including branching out and using their knowledge outside of the organization. For that purpose, a special discussion session had been arranged at Alice's home. As the group settled down, Alice introduced the subject for discussion.

"What I want to do today," she stated, "is focus on what we have accomplished, how we got there, and how we can take advantage of our learning. Anyone can start."

The Production Manager volunteered to open the discussion. With a slight grin, he said, "I'll tell you what I learned. There was a lot I didn't know about this stuff. When we committed to improving quality, improving productivity . . . you know . . . all the things we tried, I thought it would be a snap. My discovery was the people working for me told me they were behind the effort. But, you know what? They didn't have the foggiest idea of how to implement."

"Did you?" Alice asked with mild sarcasm.

"Probably not," was his honest answer. "My crossroads came when we were going for that productivity record in March. For eighteen glorious days, we were 20 percent ahead of anything we had ever done. Then we discovered that we had missed specifications on half the product made in the second week. We weren't off by much, but when we found out, the whole plant knew. I have to admit, my first reaction was to let all products go. Most customers would never have noticed. But then I started to think. What would I do to our quality effort? So, as you know, I made them rerun the bad stuff. It killed us in March, but it has paid dividends ever since. They know we're serious now."

"Especially when you made the operators scrap the bad material," the Customer Service Manager interjected.

"Right," the Production Manager responded. "People will do that once, but they hate to have fellow workers see them bale up their mistakes. But you know, I felt bad about that because they didn't mean to run bad material. They were trying for the production record, too."

The Sales Manager nodded her assent. "I suppose my crossroads came when I had to deal with Dave Henrickes. He kept bad-mouthing what we were trying. It was simply awful. When I took the time to visit his customers, I was shocked. They had no idea what our commitment to quality was all about or what it meant to them. Each one of the buyers I talked to was lining up another source. In fact, I truly believe Dave was planning on establishing himself as a broker and representing another company. My hardest decision was when he refused to come around. He kept telling me he was not about to change, didn't believe our quality effort would work, and we should just get manufacturing in shape."

"Remember when we showed him that half of his orders had mistakes in them?" the Customer Service Manager asked. "He tried to deny it, even when the specs were in his own handwriting. The man was a disaster."

"But he had a lot of sales," the Sales Manager said with a sigh. "I just wasn't sure if we could hold the business without Dave."

"We've done better," said Alice. "Those buyers were looking for someone more professional. They were under pressure from their bosses to show more value from suppliers. Dave wasn't giving them anything but a low price. That's not the way to sell in today's market."

"You started by saying you wanted us to focus on what we've accomplished," the Accounting Manager said. After shuffling through some papers, she placed an overhead slide on the projector. With a flick of the switch, the last twenty-four months' results sprang onto the wall between the sofa and Alice's desk. "Our sales have been climbing steadily at 9 percent. Our returns are virtually nil, about .001 percent for the year, but zero for the last quarter."

"On-time deliveries are 99.8 percent," the Production Manager said with a smile.

"And productivity is up," the Accounting Manager agreed. "Our units per hour are up 21 percent, and waste hit a new low last month. I have to give credit, our yields have never been better."

"That's because we have better raw materials," came the response from the Senior Buyer. "Show them the chart on our supplier ratings."

The financial and productivity results chart disappeared, replaced by a chart depicting the six suppliers of the five most-used raw materials.

"Look at metal," the Senior Buyer encouraged. "See how we went to two sources, and look at the results. I remember when they all told me we couldn't get anyone to meet our new specifications. That was my crossroads. I could have quit then, but look what happened. We're getting 99 percent plus within our spec."

The Production Manager suppressed a sarcastic remark and volunteered, "And that's how we got the extra pieces from each operator. They could count on getting good material, and they responded with more throughput. You know, they tell me they actually feel better at the higher levels of output than when we spent a lot of time standing around wondering what had to be done with all the junk we were trying to process."

The Senior Buyer nodded agreement. "You know Alice, this is where we can take advantage of our learning. Why don't we bring all of our major suppliers in here and put on a little seminar to tell them what we learned? We could share with them what we went through, and they can tell us what they are doing. We can work together to improve."

"And discuss what it takes to stick with the effort," added the Sales Manager, "and overcome your own culture."

"I don't know," the Customer Service Manager said hesitatingly. "What can we tell them that they don't already know? Some of them are much bigger than us. We could embarrass ourselves."

The Senior Buyer persisted, "We could use each other as sounding boards. Talk about what worked or didn't work. We could discuss partnering together. We give them the opportunity for a bigger share of our business, and they give us some extra values we aren't getting. We certainly can go over how we made improvements in areas outside of the plant—in order entry, billing errors, spec changes . . . you know, all that office stuff."

Alice liked the idea. "If we truly partner, we should be willing to share information that we usually withhold. We should link them with our customers . . . "

The discussion moved at a lively pace until the Customer Service, Production, and Sales Managers were commissioned to draw up an outline of how to pursue what they had learned with a select group of suppliers and how to move into a partnering relationship with a few members of that group.

During the next six months, the concepts this subgroup developed were tested with a few willing suppliers. After this testing, the subgroup picked its largest-volume raw material as the product with which to begin applying the concept of supplier partnering.

The first step was to contact each of the current six suppliers of that material to indicate the subgroup's intentions. During these contacts, it was clearly stated through a uniform message that sourcing on the material would be reduced to a maximum of two suppliers. Each supplier was to attend a briefing session, conducted by the subgroup, that would detail the philosophy behind partnering, allow suppliers to respond, solicit supplier input on any facet of the proposed long-term alliance, and establish the time frame for response.

The Production Manager assured the suppliers that their advice was sincerely invited and that any changes—for either party—that made sense for the partnering alliance would be considered. The Customer Service Manager requested that suppliers also indicate what the buyer could do to help the relationship. Assurances were given by the Sales Manager that the relationship would be far more open than in the past and that data previously restricted to suppliers would be available.

"That means," the Production Manager added, "that you will have access not just to our sales forecasts but to our operating data, shipments, inventories, and usages. We want the partnering supplier to become part of our manufacturing process."

"In body, or in spirit?" one supplier asked.

"In both," was his response. "Up to and including an office in our building, if that makes sense. We have to have access to your representative as though he or she were working directly for us. In exchange, we offer you up to 100 percent of our volume, better information, a willingness to listen to your ideas and improvement suggestions, access to previously closed data files, and a chance to maintain your position on a long-term basis."

"Moreover," the Sales Manager interjected, "if we work together to find extra values, a key feature we expect to pursue with partnering suppliers, we will share the benefits of those values."

Within two weeks following these orientation meetings, the suppliers made their "partnering" presentations to Alice's managers. Present at these sessions were representatives of the rank-and-file, those members of Alice's organization who would actually use the supplied material. Each supplier discussed its response in the form of a business proposal for the total demand for the material, emphasizing areas of potential improvement for both parties.

A typical presentation included pricing, delivery, quality, and service features, with details on quality assurance and quick response to customer needs. The sections that generated the most interest were "special values"—innovative features that could have mutual economic benefit—and "supplier needs"—elements that the suppliers wanted from the customer as conditions of the partnering agreement. In particular, the suppliers seemed interested in being involved much earlier in the design of new products.

Based on these presentations, awards were made for 75 percent and 25 percent of the business to the two organizations making the most credible and exciting proposals. A joint value-enhancement team was established with both suppliers. These teams were designed to include representatives from a cross section of both organizations, including hourly and salaried personnel. The charter for these teams was to seek additional benefits anywhere in the organizational network.

Within one year of this arrangement, the quality index on the incoming material had improved by 33 percent. Returns and allowances were cut in half on finished product delivered. Cycle time on new product introduction had been cut in half. The value-enhancement teams had found a million dollars of extra saving, which had been split between the parties.

Sharing in Trust

W. Edwards Deming (1982) lists fourteen requirements for a business to remain competitive. Requirement number four states, "End the practice of awarding business on the basis of price tag. Instead, minimize total cost. Move toward a single supplier for any one item, on a long-term relationship of loyalty and trust" (p. 23). These words may seem unrealistic to an American buyer, who is far more accustomed to the confrontational, zero-sum situation that characterizes many business negotiations in this country. To the contrary, the message is quite realistic. These words point the way toward stronger relationships than normal between buyers and sellers.

At a Toyota assembly plant, the facility will be ringed by single-source suppliers, reliably delivering goods under contract, just-in-time, totally within specification, so the manufacturing process functions smoothly with absolutely minimum inventory. These suppliers operate under the Ohno (1986) philosophy that cost has to be set to meet price and profit constraints. Then both parties—the buyer and the seller—work to reduce that cost so the supplier can enhance margin and the buyer can remain viable and competitive. The concern for buying leverage is now secondary to the interest in improving the fortunes of both buyer and seller.

Japanese firms operating in the United States attempt to follow the same approach but are often criticized because they seem to favor imported parts from Japan. This situation is a clear example of the extent to which the Japanese carry their belief in the partnering philosophy and their unyielding dedication to quality. When queried on this use of imported parts, the Japanese reply is quick and crisp: the reliability of the imported parts is so superior, their manufacturing process would suffer if inferior parts were substituted from local vendors. Japanese buyers we spoke with indicated they will buy locally when their quality requirements are met on a consistent basis.

Deming and the Japanese have proven that partnering will work. It requires dedication, practice, and patience in transforming the interaction into a profitable reality. It should be mentioned that the Japanese evolution took nearly twenty years to achieve the status their manufacturers now enjoy. What characterized that evolution was staying power and

Japanese unwillingness to forsake a philosophy that made sense.

Those still committed to the opposite perspective—having multiple suppliers vying on a price-oriented competitive basis—miss the logic that supports Deming's fourth point. Awarding business solely on the basis of price does little to enhance reliability, quality, service, or long-term loyalty. The seller may sincerely promise those features, but the seller's supporting system (plant, equipment, distributors, and so on) will lack the dedication to make it a reality. Trust under these circumstances becomes a commodity to win, not something to develop between buyer and supplier. The supplier has little incentive to improve, only to sustain supply. In addition, whenever any opportunity arises to regain margins given away in the price-cutting exercise, the supplier's people will secretly raise the buyer's costs. In Japan, the theory is to allow the supplier to make a reasonable profit while enjoying continuity of position. Then the parties work in a mutual fashion to improve margins on both sides. That situation can only exist and prosper if both parties "share in trust," or develop what Deming calls "a long-term relationship of loyalty and trust" (1982, p. 23).

Once, when Deming was asked about choosing suppliers, he advised his audience against dealing with suppliers that did not use statistical methods. Today, that advice could translate to not dealing with suppliers that do not employ some form of on-going total quality management and real-time statistical process control. The purpose is to ensure that the product supplied will meet the high demands of current markets. To the Japanese, this Deming caveat has come to mean: negotiate with suppliers to ensure availability of the right materials, delivered in the right quantities at the right time, at a competitive price, and without variability that cannot be handled by the conversion process. In the service world, this means that all the support functions are carried out with the same emphasis on reliability and customer satisfaction.

Most companies spend more on materials and services

than all other expenses combined. For this reason, costs must be controlled on these incoming commodities. The answer is to create supplier relationships in the spirit of trust and sharing of resources. In this sense, purchasing becomes more than the process of buying materials and services. It becomes the vehicle for establishing the quality and flow of incoming products and services from qualified suppliers in a partnering atmosphere. In this way, buyers ensure that the operating parameters of the business are met at the crucial first stage. Done properly, both supplier and buyer continually improve the relationship and mutually establish a competitive advantage.

We argue that the traditional purchasing concept must be expanded to operate under new paradigms and parameters:

- Supplier evaluation and selection must be examined to ensure that chosen sources are supplier-friendly to the entire organization. Potential suppliers should be encouraged to meet with departments other than purchasing to work out improvements in the supplied product or service that go beyond the question of price.
- Bidding practices should be challenged to make certain a price-only philosophy does not predominate.
- Quality must be fully guaranteed by an on-going quality management process that is ingrained in the processes of the supplier. Incoming inspection of goods should be unnecessary, and the supply of services must meet customer satisfaction demands.
- The concepts of JIT have to be understood and practiced, including quick setups, small lot sizes, on-time delivery, correct quantities, and as close to zero inventories as possible. In the service arena, that requirement equates to having the necessary number of personnel with appropriate attitudes and demeanor to deal with customer issues.
- Electronic data interchange has to be a reality, so paperwork and its inherent errors are driven to zero.

In brief, the new purchasing department has to become the center for controlling incoming quality and productivity. It must do this at costs commensurate with what is available in the market for high-caliber goods and services, with a value incentive that caps those costs and drives them lower. The major tool for this department is the long-term, flexible contract that guarantees delivery of the required commodities at a fair price. It is through long-term alliances that an environment characterized by sharing in trust will be established. Then buyers and sellers can share business strategies, growth objectives, manufacturing and services needs, and the means to enhance both's profitability.

For those who still prefer the traditional purchasing concept—forcing as much of the cost of doing business on suppliers as possible—we point out that all costs are eventually borne by the customer. That is the reality of a profit and loss statement. If a firm remains profitable, then all costs have been passed on to consumers, in some manner. It is better to know how that is done, in a partnering manner, than to suddenly realize that the costs have been carefully hidden, resulting in a competitive disadvantage.

For example, if a buyer presumes that a supplier is carrying all necessary inventories at no cost to the buyer, that is a dangerous assumption. If another supplier to a competitive buyer finds a way to meet the process needs without inventory, the second buyer-seller network has a competitive advantage. If the first network goes through an annual bidding, qualifying, and rebidding procedure when the second network has passed onto an electronic business information system, the advantage becomes even greater. If the first network trims the cost of the product supplied to the point where there are no funds for investment or innovation and the second network establishes a fixed portion of the acceptable margin for development of better products, the ultimate advantage again goes to the second network. Eventually, the long-term relationship of the second network will outperform the traditional relationship. Sharing in trust will lead the alliance network to an unbeatable advantage.

Evolution of Partnering with Suppliers

Figure 8.1 depicts our interpretation of how buyer-seller partnering can become a reality through an evolution that transcends the typical American-style bargaining process. As we consider the model depicted in that figure, we recognize that, unquestionably, there are buyer-seller networks that foster long-term quality relationships. These groups may find that our depiction does not properly describe their situation or how the parties arrived at their current position. Our purpose here is to review the partnering evolution from start to conclusion (where both parties attain a competitive advantage). In the process, we consider the pitfalls that can divert either party from successfully concluding the correct type of alliance. We salute those networks that have achieved success and avoided these potential obstacles and commend them for the market advantages they must have attained. For the others, we offer our six-stage model.

Stage 1: Uncertainty; Cultural Inhibitions

At the beginning, we find the buyer and seller far apart. Each party is uncertain about how honest the negotiation effort will be and how mutual benefit can actually accrue. Since most buyers already have a network of reasonably reliable suppliers, their offering of business necessitates that the potential new source go through a qualification or selection process. In this courtship stage, the supplier has little or no history with the buyer, so historical performance elsewhere will be offered as an inducement, with references made to semidocumented successes for other customers. Cultural inhibitions are real obstacles, as individuals in the buyer's organization are accustomed to dealing with existing suppliers and may want to disqualify the potential, new supplier.

Figure 8.1. Evolution of Buyer-Supplier Partnering.

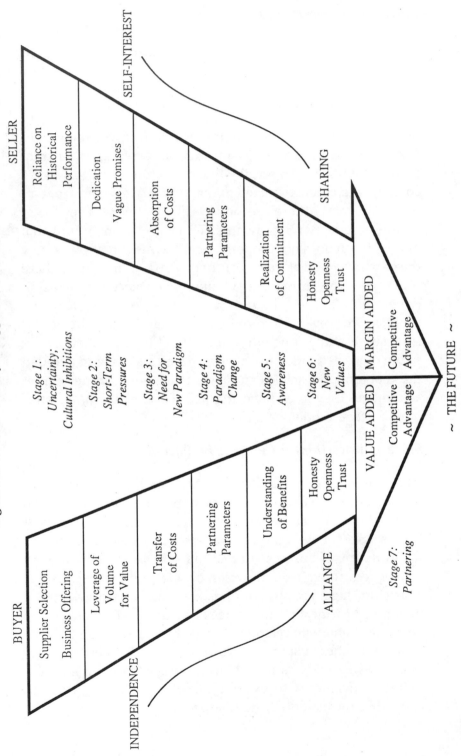

Stage 2: Short-Term Pressures

If the relationship persists into the second stage, the buyer will sense whether a qualified supplier is sincerely soliciting a position and may offer a volume opportunity for values not currently received. From the buyer's perspective, this move is tantamount to leveraging the chance for new business against the seller's willingness to make a response, usually a price cut. From the seller's perspective, there will be a need to at least feign dedication or risk bringing the courtship to an abrupt ending. With the understanding that existing suppliers already share the volume position and will be disposed to react to hold those positions, the pricing reaction and any other promises will tend to be vague.

In this early stage, there are short-term pressures at work that could influence the budding relationship. The buyer will be under pressure to hold the line on costs or to meet some programmed cost-improvement objective. The seller will be pressured for new business to meet the always budgeted increase in volume. The relationship will remain cautious, as the buyer has already existing sources and the seller has existing accounts from which it may be easier to show growth than to try to establish new relationships.

Stage 3: Need for New Paradigm

The third stage is characterized by classical negotiation. The buyer will exercise the position of controlling the orders in exchange for transfer of existing costs to the supplier. The simplest transfer is exacting a price concession, so the buyer's direct cost is reduced. Discounts, allowances for freight, better terms, carrying of inventory, and promotional and advertising allotments are other less-direct methods, but the result is the same. Costs are moved from the buyer's profit and loss statement to the supplier's. The seller, now more anxious to secure the preferred business because of the investment in time, preparation costs, and effort, becomes more ready to absorb those costs.

At this point, the traditional courtship process can be consummated or canceled. Or both parties can start to realize there are extra values to be gained from exercising a different set of principles. In the former instance (the traditional process), the prevailing reality is that the business will remain with the incumbent suppliers, probably at lower prices. Unless a substantial cost transfer occurs, the incumbents retain position. In the latter instance, however, the conversation moves toward an enduring and mutually rewarding relationship. For whatever reason, one or both parties may sense that there has to be a better way to do business. There should be a new paradigm describing the relationship between buyers and sellers that makes better sense. Unless new paradigms are realized and enacted, the outcome is business as usual. The margins on the business will be shaved, leaving the incumbent supplier to find other hidden ways to offset the absorbed cost. The incentive for innovation will be dampened, and innovation will now have to come from the buyer's marketing and sales departments, rather than from the seller's desire to bring added values to a loyal buyer. The drive for quality will slide, requiring reinforcement by the buyer's manufacturing and quality group, since the seller's organization will be disposed to get by with minimal extra effort due to the thinner margins on the business. This is not partnering. This is traditional myopic, tubular thinking at work. The result is a weaker network supplying commercially accepted quality at a lower price, and no real self-generating incentive for providing added values or helping the buyer's manufacturing or conversion process.

Stage 4: Paradigm Change

The fourth stage is the most difficult transition level. Both sides must exercise their learning and dedication to forge a different, mutually beneficial relationship. Unfortunately, this learning is often superficial at first, possibly driven by senior management rather than fashioned by the buyer and seller. Testing will undoubtedly be necessary and should be carried out to prove the validity of the emerging principles that will eventually create the new alliance. The first requirement is the acceptance of this partnering axiom:

> *Absorbing costs within a buyer-seller network instead of working together to eliminate those costs is not a true advantage to the buyer. It puts the network at a competitive disadvantage relative to a more resourceful arrangement.*

Returning to the concept of trust, that ingredient has to be seeded in this fourth stage. The primary benefits of trust have to be clearly delineated and understood. These benefits can initially accrue to the buyer, in exchange for a fair return to the supplier. Eventually, benefits must be shared, or the definition of partnering is violated. One particular aspect of the new network illustrates our point. The JIT demands will need close scrutiny in the beginning to make certain the right promises are kept by the supplier. At the same time, the buyer's organization has to begin a serious effort to improve the forecasts given to the supplier. We find far more information on usage and demand is available than finds its way into the typical buyer's projected needs.

The Japanese have progressed JIT to a *kanban* system, where knowledge is so thorough, just the right amount of the right product is delivered in time for use. In the United States, buyers and sellers have to shed old thinking to begin discussing the terms of alliances that are taken for granted in Japan. As a simple example, quality control in Japan means variability is reduced because a single source supplies all of one product, made totally within specification. In the United States, quality control means inspectors cull out or report on the number of defects per supplier, each of which has a different variability. In the worst case, that variability shows up at jammed machines or in rework areas. Meanwhile, the supplier's costs are higher than necessary because of the culled-out rejects that got shipped but should never have been produced.

The paradigm change we seek is from the traditional emphasis on price, quantity, and delivery to quality, just-in-time, and *kaizen* (continuous improvement). Such a shift will challenge the most dedicated of organizations. To meet these new objectives, both sides need to alter their perspective. The supplier has to have an internal house in order, people who understand quality, and a system to sustain and improve current performance. There must be a meaningful improvement policy reflected in everything that is done. It should be possible to select someone from any level in this type of organization who knows how to help the customer.

The buyer's change will be from a position that uses volume leverage for concessions to one that shares volume for added values. This is the more difficult alteration. Gross (1989, p. 4) puts the matter in succinct terms when he states: "In general, most of the events that occur as an industry matures tend to create more options for buyers, gradually increasing their relative power. A buyer with power to improve his position relative to suppliers will only rarely leave that power unused indefinitely in the name of fairness. Eventually he will exert his power."

If the buyer cannot change viewpoints, the potential alliance will not progress to the next stage of our model. So long as the buyer exercises the leverage of volume for price concessions, there can be no real partnering, no shared alliance. The traditions of the mature market will prevail. Business partnering seeks a set of conditions beyond the typical, mature leverage—a new arrangement that ensures future viability. The new paradigm becomes:

Providing the goods and services that are necessary to sustain the business at competitive prices. This provision

> *is made so that the supplier makes a reasonable profit and the buyer can sell to the ultimate consumer at competitive levels knowing there will be a continuous flow of shared improvements.*

Stage 5: Awareness

Continuing with our model in Figure 8.1, the buyer and seller who truly want to build a meaningful, long-term, competitive alliance must shift from independence and self-interest to a trust that leads to sharing and partnering. Moving to the fifth stage requires a full awareness of the eventual commitments that will be required. The buyer can now sense the additional benefits that can accrue from adoption of the new paradigm. The goal becomes securing higher levels of performance and innovation to better meet the customer's needs. Buyers clearly see their role as the catalyst to achieve that goal. For the seller, it also becomes crucial to realize the extent of the commitment being made. Promises not kept at this stage can doom both parties. Win-win for both parties suddenly takes on real meaning.

To illustrate the activities that transpire in the fifth stage, we describe an actual proposal we made to a major customer. This firm, representing a large national-brand consumer product, approached us (as the supplier) along the traditional lines we have described. Initially, the firm emphasized price concessions on our part in exchange for what amounted to an opportunity for us to increase our existing volume position from $2 million annual sales to $8 million. We suggested to the buyer that a new paradigm would allow us to bring savings to the arrangement that would greatly exceed typical pricing concessions. We proposed that the buyer allow us to bring a team inside the customer's operations to look for savings in areas that would traditionally be restricted to personnel working for the customer.

At Stage 5, we negotiated a series of mutual actions that

would lead to these savings. The customer agreed to allow us to send a team of professionals (hourly and salaried) into their operations to seek, in concert with the customer's local personnel, potential improvements in *any* area of their operations. The target established for this action team was 10 percent cost improvement. The team that went into the customer's facility developed savings just under $2,000,000. Since the target was set at $8,000,000 × .10 or $800,000, the target was exceeded by 2½X.

Stage 6: New Values

In the sixth stage, the alliance is finally coming together. The new values being discussed, tested, reviewed, modified, and solidified are run through the gamut of evaluation. These values include team searches for improvements to any phase of the process. Such action could entail a jointly conducted operational analysis, joint team problem solving, joint investment in equipment, focused facilities created to reduce inventory and cycle times, and so forth. Now the proposed partnering has to reflect an honesty, openness, and trust that is atypical of the traditional relationship. Financial data may be shared that would previously only be seen at the highest management level. Business plans will be opened on both sides. Strategies that have dual meaning will be forged. Traditional paper-intense systems will give way to electronic linkages that have access, in some instances, to internal cost data.

Both organizations will be interfacing, not just within the buyer-seller area, but from rank-and-file to senior management. Mutual success will be the theme as representatives from this vertical slice of the alliance spend time together identifying and working out solutions to strengthen the partnering. Each side becomes far more aware of what factors will result in success for the emerging network. That means they understand the interactive process from raw material through ultimate consumption of the product or service. Continuous improvement and the importance of the alliance for competitive advantage become the major points of conversation.

Stage 7: Partnering

The alliance is truly forged in the seventh stage. The buyer receives a stream of added value from consistent quality, faster response time, flexible manufacturing, lower inventories, shorter cycle times, and innovative enhancements. The seller receives the continuity of larger orders, better forecasts, specification changes that positively affect productivity, and the added margins accruing through shared savings discovered by the value-improvement teams. Both organizations have cemented the relationship in the name of competitive advantage. The alliance necessary to secure the future for both parties has been created.

Reality or Myth

The reader may be wondering: does supplier partnering exist? Or is it a myth? Our response, based on experience, direct interviews with organizations practicing some form of this partnering, and analysis of available data, is that it is developing on many fronts, but only a small number of organizations have made it happen. At present, the intentions are great, the number of trial situations is growing, favorable results are being reported, but there is more hope than reality. It remains for more organizations to show the necessary perseverance for partnering to become institutionalized.

Organizations that are experimenting with some form of business partnering do have the basic ingredients to progress to the point of mutual competitive advantage. The buyer must move forcefully, but with understanding, patience, and perseverance, toward those issues that will bring the nontraditional extra values to the relationship. This effort must be endorsed and supported throughout the buyer's organization, and the effort has to be conducted with suppliers that share the same philosophy. Two elements are critical to making the effort a reality:

- The purchasing role must be elevated to one of determining the requisite quality for further processing throughout the buyer's organization.
- The purchasing function must seek values, while building a network of suppliers in a partnering atmosphere, that is, the buyer must also act like a good customer and share, as well as receive, in the relationship.

We have argued that business partnering is a today tool — designed to garner a competitive advantage in today's marketplace. The problem with all tools lies in their potential misuse. Used properly, partnering enhances the "pull-through" capability of a supplier-buyer-customer network. That means organizations and their people work in a mutual manner to pull products and services of more satisfying value through the interworking system to the ultimate consumer, with a reasonable profit for all constituents. Used improperly, partnering could become a faddish phenomenon with little substance, meaning only that one party has overleveraged another.

We are enthusiastic on the potential of the concept, but our investigation of current practices forces us to recommend caution in accepting many of the purported success stories. After a literature search on partnering and scores of interviews with practicing professionals, one conclusion dominates our analysis. Most partnering efforts have been exercises conducted by large buyers to force quality and price concessions on willing suppliers, giving little to the supplier other than large volume positions. While most purchasing professionals avow the validity of the partnering concepts, they defend the volume for quality and cost trade-off and express mixed reactions about the feasibility of partnering. They prefer the traditional methodology of leveraging orders for concessions rather than showing a willingness to experiment with what they admit is the logic behind partnering. There certainly exists a growing body of advocates for reducing supplier bases, with larger shares of business in exchange for added value. But there is a definite reluctance to move into the mutual sharing aspects required for true partnering to exist.

Closer relationships with "world-class suppliers" has a solid ring to it, but our search found more sloganeering than substantial, shared interaction. The reality starts with the certification of the supplier base by the buyer. Criteria and rating systems have sprung into existence to evaluate and monitor a supplier's capabilities and performance. The more exacting of these systems include site visits, employee interviews, documentation of control systems, training, and ongoing use of statistical methods and total quality assurance. Rewards, along with increasing shares of business, are meted out to those who meet the criteria. Vendor-of-the-period awards are becoming more common. Levels of certification are now segregating the good-better-best suppliers. While many of these early alliances have been accompanied by marked progress in performance, very few qualify as successful partnering efforts. They fail to meet the mutual benefit criterion.

Typically, the supplier in the alliance does receive a larger share of business. The question of whether or not that increased share also raises profit, however, depends on the pricing concessions or cost transfers exacted during the negotiating process. The buyer will also receive commitments for quality and service performance that should lower costs and enhance the buyer's manufacturing or service process. The question of whether or not these commitments will be met depends on factors within the supplier's process that might negate the promises offered in exchange for extra business. In brief, the whole process is threatened with unintentional fraud because of conditions that neither party will completely fulfill.

As an example, consider a firm that very faithfully creates

a supplier-rating system with the honest intention of partnering with fewer suppliers, the ones that can best meet the rating criteria. Consider next what happens to a long-time source with good connections that cannot meet an essential measure, for example, on-time deliveries. If that source is kept on for an extended time while other sources that can consistently deliver on time fail to improve their positions, the measurement and criteria exist in name only. At the same time, if a supplier realizes getting a certain grade on the rating system is essential to securing new business, there is a strong temptation to temporarily achieve the required mark without really changing the process to achieve high performance on a sustained basis. The missing ingredient to these alliances is the mutual search for permanent solutions to benefit both supplier and buyer.

Mindful of these limitations, some organizations are attempting to move their supplier evaluation systems to a more effective level. Black & Decker, the tool and appliance manufacturer, has been developing a process that features ratings on quality, technology, delivery, and commercial aspects. Roger P. Sterling, vice-president for global purchasing, reports the system has quantitative measures specific to a particular plant's needs. Black & Decker now plans to expand the system to more parts of the corporation (Roger P. Sterling, personal communication, March 1991). Black & Decker and others are now moving to help suppliers legitimately improve performance in critical areas. This type of focused effort is necessary to attain the mutual benefit requirement of partnering. Done effectively, the focus will also reveal techniques from the buyer's side that can benefit supplier performance—an issue generally shunned in many so-called partnering alliances.

Kenneth Stork (Cayer, 1991), corporate director of materials and purchasing for Motorola, adds an important postscript to the evolving certification procedures. He counsels that worse than using rating systems without appropriate follow-up procedures is the practice of many companies (buyers) demanding more from their suppliers than they do from their own manufacturing operations. As we have noted, such practice defeats the partnering intention and reduces the association to the traditional leveraging of volume for cost transfers.

With perseverance, the supplier certification process can lead to meaningful results. Campbell Soup Company has been developing its "Select Supplier Program" for almost five years. Although Steve K. Parker, director of procurement, reports they were frustrated by the slow supplier response at first, they have achieved successes in some traditional commodity areas (personal communication, December 17, 1990). Featured in the Campbell program are employee team exchanges, sharing of traditionally confidential information, and multiyear contracts. The partnering alliance between Campbell and Nippon Steel is a shining example of what can be accomplished. As part of the certification process, Nippon supplied organizational charts listing names and defining responsibilities of those who affected the process that would deliver hot band can stock. Flowcharts were added indicating who to contact for any type of help that might be required. Measurement charts verifying that all product supplied was within specification were included. Labor productivity data were supplied showing significant progress on increasing yields and productivity per employee. Such information is rarely shared among U.S. companies.

When Campbell had to reject one roll of hot band in eighteen months, it received a very unusual response. The replacement roll was sent to the appropriate Campbell site. In addition, letters from the involved Nippon employees were sent to Campbell, fully explaining what had happened to create the reject roll and what each employee would do to make certain it would not happen in the future. This type of supplier response is one reason Nippon is now a major Campbell source.

John Pughe (1990) of Allied Corporation presented the positive aspects that can develop with true supplier partnering. Speaking at a roundtable discussion he said, "We want to develop a wholesome relationship with our suppliers. We want them to understand our market and where we want to be in that market. We take suppliers right into our forecasting module so they can read what our requirements are: what the first six months are, what's tentative for the next six months, and what our planning is for the next two to three years. We want to rely on them to keep us competitive and put components right into the assembly line to save us the cost of incoming or receiving inspection labor."

Such a philosophy has to lead to a stronger supplier base. We would extend this philosophy to say, "and we will also work with our suppliers to see what we can do as a customer to enhance their profits by improving their productivity and quality"; then the loop will be completed and true partnering can begin. Under these conditions, the supplier-buyer-customer network will receive the overall best of quality, cost, and service—the ingredients that establish an unbeatable competitive advantage. As a closing example, General Electric (1991) presented such an integration when it discussed its version of supplier partnering. Titled "Global Excellence—Through Applied Productivity Partnering" (GE-TAPP), General Electric announced a "structured approach to involve our suppliers in the generation and implementation of a productivity project." Long a leader in the quality pursuit, GE is now moving to strengthen its supplier base while enhancing its total network for productivity and quality.

Action Study: Sears Canada

In January 1987, Sears Canada introduced what it believed was the first supplier partnering effort in the retail sales industry, calling its system the Supplier Quality Partnership (SQP) Program. The objectives were to eliminate costly waste, help the company secure a competitive edge in the global market, and motivate Sears Canada and its supplier network to implement Total Quality Management. The program was expected to be influential and generate important results since the company was purchasing about $3 billion of annual product from over 4,000 suppliers.

The most interesting part of Sears Canada's effort was that at the outset, "all of these suppliers told us [Sears Canada] that they had quality" (Gordon, 1990, p. 41). These assurances were contradicted by the fact that the company was experiencing an increasing return rate. In fact, while suppliers were making positive pronouncements about quality, the Quality Department at Sears Canada was expressing concern about the increasing number of catalogue returns and difficulties with suppliers. Something was obviously wrong, and SQP was launched to help cope with the problems. The decision was made to incorporate the International Standards Organization 9000 (a set of international quality standards that establish basic parameters for a quality assurance process), international quality standards, and several recognized quality specifications into what became their *Supplier Quality Guide.*

This guide was established to "identify the elements of the Supplier Quality System that must be planned, developed, implemented, and maintained by suppliers to provide for the:

- Reliable detection of incoming and in-process discrepancies;
- Control and timely, positive disposition of nonconforming items;
- Implementation of corrective actions to prevent recurrence of nonconformancies;
- Timely delivery of products and services that meet requirements all the time;
- Measurement of the cost of nonconformance, appraisal, prevention—and the savings due to improvement" (Gordon, 1990, p. 43).

In the pilot phase of the program introduction, twenty-four sources were selected, based on recommendations from the Sears Canada buyers, to participate in a six-month study designed to help implement SQP. All twenty-four sources assured the company: "we have control of our quality, and we know what we are doing" (p. 44). An initial audit of this pilot group contradicted these statements:

- 80 percent had no written quality policies/procedures
- 75 percent had no control on nonconformance
- 71 percent had no corrective action procedures
- 58 percent had no control of subsuppliers
- 54 percent had no quality commitments by the CEO/president

Additional weaknesses were found in delegation of responsibilities, processing of defective incoming materials, late deliveries, poor documentation, and the belief that improving quality increases costs. A revealing quote by Niall Gordon stated, "Although many of our sources blamed their suppliers for defects found in completed product, few had formal receiving inspection programs to prevent the adding of value to defective products" (1990, p. 45).

The next complication Sears Canada encountered was selling the program to its own buyers. The initial reaction of that group was one of skepticism. To overcome this negative reaction, the quality group set about to prove that suppliers could meet requirements. Seven hundred and fifty-eight suppliers of 78 percent of Sears Canada's purchased products were selected as a priority group. This pilot group was expanded to include subsuppliers since incoming material was the leading problem, according to the primary suppliers. Most of these subsources informed Sears Canada that they "were already doing the best we can" and that "no one in our industry is doing any better" (1990, p. 47).

The SQP program is another lesson in the value of perseverance. Sears Canada insisted that reluctance be overcome and the process go forward. Some of the results are astounding:

- 80 percent reduction in defects identified by customer complaints
- Internal rejects down 50 percent on soft lines (for example, clothes)
- 47 percent reduction in seconds on hard lines (for example, tools, appliances)
- 21 percent increase in profits
- 47 percent reduction in customer returns on soft lines

Perhaps more important, Sears Canada proved what can be accomplished with a concerted focus on supplier partnering. Sears Canada now deals with companies involved in their own quality improvement processes, where before there was no evidence of any quality systems. The company has also seen favorable changes in its own internal quality capability. For Sears Canada, continuing the SQP program "has become a necessary way of doing business" (1990, p. 49).

Summary

After there are sufficient internal alliances in place to ensure that tenets of the improvement process are being met and sustained, the next step is external partnering, and the logical place to begin external partnering is with suppliers. Indeed, supplier partnering is happening. Unfortunately, in most cases the reality is that only a partial form of partnering is being enacted. The majority of current partnerings are characterized by buyers leveraging their purchasing position for cost absorption by suppliers. Under such conditions, only one party can reap the benefits and enhance its competitive advantage.

True supplier partnering requires an understanding of each party's needs and capabilities to establish a clear vision for focusing the efforts of people who work for buyer and supplier. Necessary improvement can then be dedicated to those areas identified as requiring attention and improvement. If that focus is placed, as it has been in most cases, solely on the buyer's perceived needs, nothing happens to establish overall improvement to the buyer-seller network. Long-term commitments then become nebulous and difficult to achieve. Continuous improvement is also reduced to a short-term project instead of an ongoing process.

The correct way to approach supplier partnering is to work in a spirit of trust with qualified sources to ascertain the true *capability* of the total supplier-to-consumer system. The next step is to focus on the *needs* of the total partnering network. The match of these two analyses then illustrates the effort that will be necessary to build competitive advantage into the alliance. This critical idea—that both organizations exist to satisfy the ultimate consumer while creating the profits necessary to sustain the network—must always be kept in mind.

Long-term partnering is encouraged as the alliance begins to demonstrate a consistency in meeting and exceeding the consumer's expectations. Trust, information sharing, more effective communications, ongoing value analyses, employee exchanges, compliance to necessary standards, forecast reliability, review process, the building of a business structure for sustaining the network, and a focus on reality instead of cosmetics become the ingredients for future success.

A good partnering situation must remain in a mode of continual improvement or the alliance will decline and perish. There can be no status quo or "savings for the moment." There are simply too many other organizations chasing the same objectives. That means each existing alliance is in some way under attack. When both parties are prepared to give as well as receive, then the alliance is capable of gaining the necessary competitive advantage. The blueprint is available. Common sense and perseverance will transform that blueprint into reality, for both supplier and buyer.

Chapter Nine

◆

BUSINESS PARTNERING
WITH CUSTOMERS

Once a business organization has established a network of internal and external suppliers with high reliability, it can move the partnering system toward the customer and the ultimate consumer. Partnering then becomes the logical outcome of a concerted network-improvement effort. The network consists of a chain of organizations working together to optimize the use of all resources required to sustain a viable system, from beginning materials and services through final consumption. Effective use of human contributions must be a consistent characteristic of that network, as should the search for continuous improvement to maintain what surely will be a competitive advantage.

What characteristics should be in place before an organization is ready to undertake customer partnering? Innovation, unyielding dedication to quality and customer satisfaction, active leadership, management by facts, lots of training, and recognition of contributors should be evident throughout the system. Delighting the customer should be key for determining levels of performance. Total quality management will have meaning throughout the network. At this enviable point of evolution, the organization is ready to go to the customer to discuss partnering for the purpose of strengthening the network and increasing its competitive advantage.

Movement to customer partnering must be approached cautiously, so the organization does not overextend itself. Our recommendation is to initiate partnering with a limited number of test customers. The first efforts should certainly be established on a pilot basis to prove the capability of the system to fulfill the commitments that will undoubtedly be made. This caution is grounded in our experience that partnering is not yet an accepted business practice and that general understanding of its premises is weak.

As we attempted to practice what we espouse about business partnering, we discovered that most forays into some type of partnering arrangement have been initiated by a buying group seeking advantages through some form of *supplier* partnering. In most instances, a buyer or buying council had put suppliers through a certification process and then offered larger-volume positions for the features discussed in the previous chapter.

When we tried to reverse the positions and proactively seek partnering alliances with *customers*, we caught most buyers and managers off guard. They were accustomed to initiating the partnering discussion by offering a position of supposedly greater value in exchange for special value enhancements. The change to partnering alliances with customers might seem trivial since most of the same characteristics of business partnering apply, regardless of the direction of the arrangement. The distinction is important, however, because moving toward the customer should only be attempted when an organization's internal house is in order and the supplier part of the network can keep all the promises that will have to be made to the customer. This position contrasts with the supplier making vague promises in response to partnering inquiries simply to gain a large-volume, long-term position. Many suppliers make such promises, we found, in the hope that the type of improvements we claim are necessary to make the alliance work successfully will be developed (a learn-as-we-go methodology). Partnering—in any direction, but especially toward the customer—should not proceed in that manner.

In essence, we suggest that external partnering moves

toward the customers backed up by a solid network of external suppliers and internal alliances. Figure 9.1 was created by
Walker Automotive, a subsidiary of Tenneco, Inc., to depict
this condition. What it refers to as the "Supplier/Walker Team"
produces the output—from a network of linked organizations—
that goes to the external customers. The products and services
are of guaranteed high quality, by virtue of the effectiveness
of the members of the team. Doing their best to ensure the
reliability of the output that moves to the customer, team members are the links to customer satisfaction from the beginning
to the end of the chain of interaction.

Figure 9.1. Walker External Supplier/Customer Chain.

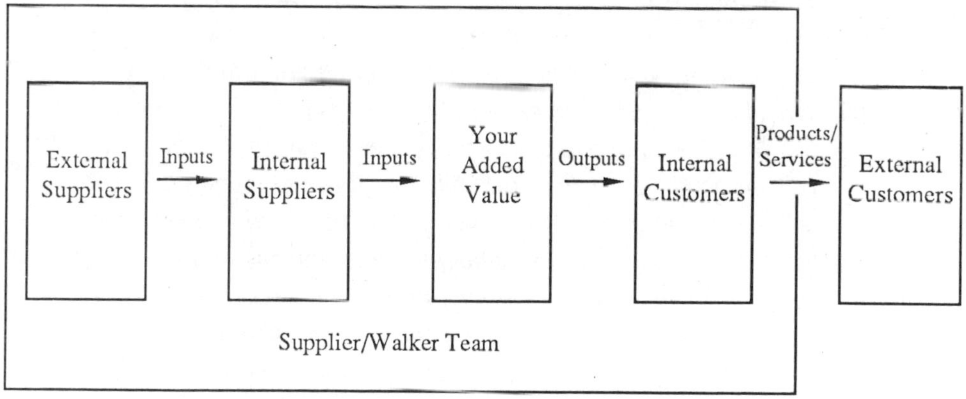

Source: Walker Manufacturing. Used by permission.

Will this type of an arrangement always guarantee success? If the format is understood and faithfully executed,
chances for success certainly improve. But certainty is determined as much by the buyer's—as well as the seller's—
intentions. Let us return again to Alice Harper as she moves
toward her customer, using the advantages gained from her
improvement effort, to seek new business on a partnering
basis.

Alice Steps Out

Alice Harper and her Sales Manager were idly discussing their game plan as they awaited the person who would escort them to their appointment with the vice-president of purchasing for Excellent Brands, the giant food conglomerate. Excellent had been a customer for some time, but Alice and her company had been invited to make a presentation for a much larger share of business as part of Excellent's "Partners in Action" program. This program had been introduced to virtually all of Excellent's suppliers via a series of seminars designed to describe how purchasing would be conducted during the next five-to-ten years.

Excellent had told its suppliers it was serious about partnering and expected to reduce its supplier base substantially—to those that rated highest on measures of quality, delivery, service, and innovation. As "partners in action," inventories were to be banished, all incoming inspection would be eliminated, all products would meet rigorous quality levels (measured by defects per million), and cycle time was to be reduced (to one-fourth of current levels). Penalties would be levied for any internal delays caused by supplier products, and any returns would have to be replaced within twenty-four hours. The rewards for the successful suppliers were to be long-term contracts with significantly larger shares of orders, up to single-source positions in some instances.

Excellent was an important customer for Alice's plant, representing 14 percent of total business. Alice and members of her staff naturally attended the Partners in Action Seminar when invited and had prepared their response to the challenges presented by the many Excellent officers who participated. "Bring us ideas," they had exhorted. "We are prepared to listen. We are not just interested in the lowest price. Tell us how we can improve. We want your honest input so we can be a better company." Each supplier had been instructed to develop a partnering plan for meeting the new requirements in exchange for enhanced volume positions.

Immediately after attending the seminar, Alice and her Sales Manager had worked up their response, based on what had been accom-

plished internally at their plant and externally with their major suppliers. They decided to base the presentation on the full potential of their people and supplier network to not only meet, but exceed, the new standards set down by Excellent.

"I'll let you do the preliminaries," Alice reminded the Sales Manager. "Then I'll go into the commitments we're prepared to make."

The Sales Manager nodded. "Just take your time. I hear they've been inundated with responses. My contact says they are already skeptical about some of the promises being made."

"I'll do that," Alice agreed. "And I won't tell them we'll do things we can't back up."

"Well, be prepared to move on the pricing."

"They told us we didn't have to focus on pricing."

"This is Excellent, Alice. They always focus on pricing. I don't care what those executives said. We're dealing with the purchasing department. Their careers depend on making budgeted cost improvements. They will want to see low prices."

Alice began to pace nervously around the coffee table covered with Excellent's internal news reports.

"They told us to bring ideas, innovations, and ways to find extra values," she protested. "That's what our plan is built around. I'm not going to tie up 30 to 40 percent of our capacity for one customer and do it at a loss."

"I'm just cautioning you that the people we see today will act like they are interested in all those good things, but unless we lay a low price on the table, they will give the business to someone else. And we'll lose our 14 percent portion."

"We'll stick with the prices in our proposal," Alice insisted. "Unless I sense they have weak interest in our ideas," she said as an afterthought.

At that moment, a person from the purchasing department arrived to escort them to the conference room where the sales presentation was to take place.

Following brief introductions, amenities, and the traditional exchange of business cards, Alice and the Sales Manager settled across the conference table from the Vice-President, the Purchasing Director, the Senior Buyer for Packaging, and a representative from Excellent's Quality Resources Department.

"Well," the Vice-President started, "did you enjoy the seminar?"

"Indeed, we did," the Sales Manager responded. "It looks like Excellent is prepared to take some bold steps, and we want to go with you. Alice and I were there, and we immediately determined that what we've been doing at our plant fits perfectly with what you want from Partners in Action."

"That's what we like to hear," the Vice-President said with a positive nod. "You stand a chance to markedly increase your volume position, if we see the advantages in doing so. It doesn't have to be rocket science, but it has to be an improvement. When our CEO said we want new ways of doing business together, we all agreed to work toward that end. So the floor is yours. We're all ears."

The Sales Manager leaned forward and established eye contact with the Vice-President. "We've already enjoyed a good relationship with Excellent. Our returns are extremely small."

"Thirteen hundred parts per million, last year," the representative from Quality Resources interrupted.

The Sales Manager maintained eye contact. "That's less than 1 percent . . . and we can do better. We've been working diligently with our people and our suppliers. We firmly believe we can get to less than 100 parts per million within twelve months. We have trained all our people on statistical process control. We have SPC implemented throughout the plant, even in the office, and with our suppliers. One of the key features of our proposal, as you will see, is to eliminate your need for incoming inspection. We will supply product totally within your specifications."

"I would like to suggest," Alice said slowly, "that one of the first steps would be to set up a joint team to determine what those specifications should be. Perhaps we can improve . . . "

"We gave you our specs," the quality representative protested, with a tinge of irritation.

"I know," Alice responded, "but your group vice-president said we could offer some changes, if they benefited both parties."

The nonresponsive scowl and defiant body language told Alice that one member of the Excellent team had not endorsed the principle of accepting outside ideas.

"Why don't we let Alice review our proposal," the Sales Manager suggested. "If we all look at the booklets we passed out, you can follow along."

"Let's do that," the Vice-President agreed and, focusing on Alice, added, "I also want to repeat what you heard at our seminar. We want to develop a network of world-class suppliers, with people who have a shared sense of values. Partners in Action is not a new tool to get more out of our suppliers. We want to hear how we can both profit, and if that means changing a few things or attacking the not-invented-here syndrome, then we'll do it."

"On that note," Alice said with a smile, "I'd like to outline how we believe we interface with the concepts of Partners in Action."

The group stirred and began to split their attention between Alice and the pages of her proposal.

"To begin," she said, "we would like to arrange for a team of our associates, hourly and salaried, to visit your facilities."

"What for?" the Purchasing Director asked spontaneously. "We don't normally allow visitors . . . unless there's a specific purpose."

"The only way we can drive home your real needs in terms meaningful to our people is to let them see firsthand what happens to our product. If I tell them poor quality causes you grief, they can discount my words as typical management rhetoric. But if they see for themselves what happens if we don't do it right or talk to your people and hear directly what they have to do to cover our mistakes, they come back actually inspired to not make those mistakes."

"Sounds good to me," the Vice-President mused.

Alice proceeded through the features of her proposal, detailing each aspect as a direct response to an intention of Excellent's Partners in Action process. Her audience was attentive and asked clarifying questions throughout her presentation. She drew heavily on her experiences with the improvement process her company had fostered and the supplier partnering effort they recently concluded.

"We think we're ready for partnering with Excellent," she summarized. "What we would like is the chance to show you what we can *do. We invite you to come see us, make a quality audit of our facilities, talk to our associates, and together we can develop an action plan."*

"Alice," the Senior Buyer responded with caution, "we have the action plan. You just have to meet the criteria. What we have is a twelve-step qualification procedure."

"I've read the procedure," Alice acknowledged, "and we will meet the requirements. But I was under the impression we could suggest ways to help both of us."

"We tried to anticipate those types of ideas," the Buyer defended. "Before we finalized that format, we talked to some of our largest suppliers . . . "

"What type of things did you have in mind, Alice?" the Vice-President asked, with a wave of silence to the Buyer.

"Well, your procedure calls for an electronic linkage. We can do that, but I'd like to suggest we do a summary billing over that system and have a funds transfer each month."

"We don't pay in thirty days," the Buyer said coolly.

"You could, and you would save money," Alice replied. "We can eliminate the errors, save the paperwork and the postage, and not have to chase down billings."

"In other words, we can help develop the relationship by changing a few of our traditions," the Vice-President said, with a grin.

Alice acknowledged the endorsement and proceeded.

"We could also get involved together much earlier as you develop new products if we had a person tied in with your R&D group. That could cut cycle time for you and give us a chance to show how minor changes can help our manufacturing process. You get faster response. We improve our processing."

"You're asking for contacts we don't normally allow," the Buyer protested. "We give the new product specifications to our suppliers after the design is tested and approved."

"I know," said Alice, "and if it doesn't fit our process, we have to delay manufacturing while we make changes. A little input ahead of time can help both of us."

"It's your job to figure out how to meet . . . ," the Purchasing Director began.

"No, it isn't," the Vice-President interrupted. "I see where you're going, Alice. You want a two-way street, and we're trying to drive you down a one-way boulevard."

Alice smiled her acknowledgment.

"I like what you're saying, and I want you to pursue the things you have in this proposal. You've shown a lot of innovation and that's good," the Vice-President complimented.

"I hope I'm not asking for anything unreasonable," Alice added. "I guess I just took your CEO seriously when we were told to be innovative."

"We want innovation," the Purchasing Director responded, "but a lot of work went into those qualification procedures. That's what I think we should focus on."

"We intend to do that," was Alice's reply. "We also want to work at this together, so we both benefit."

The Vice-President smiled and commented, "Seems like you also want us to carry our load, too."

"Only seems fair," Alice said, with a smile.

The meeting continued for a while as all participants concentrated on searching for values that could make the arrangement a win-win situation for both parties. The meeting concluded with the Vice-President telling Alice and her Sales Manager, "You look like an organization that has captured what we're searching for. We want long-term relationships with organizations that share our values. Give us a chance to review what you presented today, and we'll advise you . . . "

"Will the decision be based on what each company presents?" Alice asked as she rose to leave.

"Yes," the Vice-President answered. "We told you this is not a game to get price concessions from our suppliers. We want lasting relationships, and cost will be just one consideration." As an afterthought, "I think you had some good ideas" was added.

One week later, the Sales Manager appeared at the door to Alice's office and said, frowning, "Well, I warned you. The buyer just called from Excellent."

"Well?" Alice waited.

"We're out. We lost the whole thing."

"How? Why? What did they say?"

"Gilroy got a second look and cut the price by 18 percent."

"Did they offer anything besides price?"

"Nope! Buyer says they got to the big boss in operations and put it all on an economical basis. Made the boss look like a hero. So word went down to place the business."

It took Alice an hour to recover from the disappointing news. When she had regained control, she placed a call to the Vice-President of Purchasing at Excellent.

"Could you give me some insight?" she asked politely. "I don't mind losing out, but I like to learn from my experiences. How could we have done better?"

"You did well," the Vice-President said with a sigh. "You just have to understand, Alice, that sometimes politics and attractive pricing get in the way of good intentions."

"I understand that," Alice replied, "but you gave us assurances that total values would be the issue, for the long term . . . "

"Alice," came the interruption. "You have to see that our company is no different from any other. There is enormous pressure at all times for cost reduction. If one of our suppliers is crazy enough to give away the store to get some volume, we have to look at it. In this case, Gilroy was afraid to lose position, and they went to the top with up-front savings. It was a case of a qualified source offering pricing well below any other bidder."

"But there isn't that kind of margin in this business. Gilroy can't eat that much of a cut and make any profit."

"That's your assumption, Alice. Maybe they have better costs."

"Maybe," Alice sighed, "but we benchmarked our improvements on the best in the business, and we're sure our costs are not out of line. It looks to me like you have a very hungry company that can't come up with those 'other values' you said you wanted."

"They had some extra features as well."

"Did they match our features?"

"Some of your ideas were very good, Alice. Some would take a long time to digest. In the long run, Gilroy will match your proposal."

Sensing there was no advantage in pursuing the matter, Alice asked, "Do we phase out of our position?"

"I'm afraid we've been told to move fast. Your orders stop next week."

"And the years of service and designs we gave in the past . . . "

"You were paid for that, Alice."

"Well, lots of luck with your new partner."

"I hope you mean that," was the concluding remark.

Alice punched in the extension number for the Sales Manager.

"Who is Excellent's biggest competitor?" she asked. *"Find out and* set up a meeting. They're about to have a lucky day."

The Partnering Network

When a business organization goes forward to partner with a customer, a primary intention should be to involve the entire system in providing customer satisfaction. That system starts with whatever organizations supply the new ingredients—whether products or services—that are transformed into consumables for the customers. Rather than being considered simply places that provide necessary ingredients, these suppliers have to be looked on as vital parts of the network. As these suppliers become stronger, better able to meet more demanding needs, and able to continuously improve those parts of their process that help the buyer, the network gets stronger. When the buying organization works as hard to improve its supplier base as it does to improve itself, the seeds of competitive advantage are sown.

A point worth stressing is that there are residual values within the supplier-to-buyer network that go largely untapped because the buyer erects a silo that says only those within the buying organization know what the specifications should be. The seller accepts that premise and dutifully supplies what the buyer requests. Ideas that could lead to valuable improvements are wasted because they are never discussed. Linking the two constituencies—supplier and buyer—closer together and encouraging discussions across various functions can only lead to enhancing the profitability of both organizations.

The focus then shifts to the link between supplier and buyer and the people who are traditionally left out of the interface—customers. The key negotiations in this area revolve, not around price, but around the process capabilities of the supplier and the process needs of the customer. That means negotiations have to go beyond buyer and sales representatives to include as many people as needed to make certain the real customer needs are understood by the supplier. Then the supplier improves the capability of the process in order to supply—and eventually to exceed—those needs to help the customer attain a competitive advantage. Xerox demonstrates this position better than most companies. For Xerox, customer requirements do not always encompass the entire universe of customer needs. So Xerox continues to match the capabilities of the Xerox process against what customers require as well as against what they may need in the future.

The consumer should be the beneficiary of a network of suppliers and customers working together to deliver the ultimate in quality and service at competitive costs. There will be numerous false starts, of course, as organizations will pretend to be interested in participating in such a network, when their real intentions are short-term financial gain. Our investigation has revealed that the field of partnering is benefiting from a few serious advocates and suffering from many companies that employ the term loosely as they pursue self-interest instead of business partnering.

Alice is ill-advised to react in anger. Her organization is primed to help customers benefit from internal improvements and an enhanced supplier network. If short-term pricing gains are chosen over systemic improvements, then she has to swallow hard and look for alliances with more serious organizations. Leveraging of volume for cost transfer is a reality of business, and those who practice the technique will find change most difficult. Alice and her Sales Manager need a 14 percent replacement to volume. If Alice dramatically reduces margin as she prices the prospective substitute volume, she will need 20–25 percent more business to replace what was lost.

Given this warning, Alice and those organizations that want to pursue customer partnering are advised to begin first with firms that are seriously seeking true partnering alliances and are willing to make such arrangements mutually beneficial. They must be alert for signs that point to overleveraging by the customer. As a start, seek customers that make a top-to-bottom commitment to share in the relationship, as opposed to those that talk about "controlling" their suppliers. Such information—and clues—appear early in the partnering brochures and communications given to prospective suppliers.

For example, Colgate-Palmolive Company introduced its partnering philosophy at a supplier conference in January, 1991. The theme of the meeting was "Realizing Our Potential—Together." Purchasing policies discussed were "develop a 'partnership' approach with suppliers who demonstrate a willingness to work supportively to lower 'total system' costs and improve mutual productivity," and "seek out and reward through business growth those suppliers who demonstrate sustained excellence in productivity and quality." Little else would be necessary if Colgate-Palmolive embraces that concept, since the essence of partnering is working supportively to lower total system costs and sustaining *excellence in productivity and quality.*

As a sign that old paradigms die hard, Colgate-Palmolive also included this policy: "develop and sustain programs in support of lowering Colgate-Palmolive's investment in inventory." The underlying logic of the statement is correct, but we would prefer to see policies that seek the elimination of the inventory in the "total system" referred to earlier. In that way, the network is strengthened, and the supplier does not interpret the policy to mean absorb inventory to please the customer. Colgate-Palmolive returns to the correct concept when it lists this requirement: "a continuing discussion of cost drivers of the supply chain is maintained which results in cooperative programs which reduce *total systems cost* [emphasis added]." Ed Fogarty, president of Colgate-Palmolive, committed to suppliers that through an "ongoing relationship based upon mutual trust, extra costs can be wrung out of the system with savings shared for mutual benefit." Therein lies the opportunity to make business partnering work. Colgate-Palmolive is obviously a viable target for a supplier serious about using the values from its improvement process for *mutual* advantage.

Always a leader in the search for world-class status, Florida Power and Light (FPL) has raised partnering to the level it deserves. In one striking example, FPL worked with Southwire, a Georgia-based supplier of underground distribution cable (1990). Southwire had prepared itself for partnering with the development of its internal improvement process called "Business Excellence." When FPL wanted to set up a pilot program to develop criteria for a vendor certification plan, Southwire was included in the early stages. Through a mutual effort, defects were continuously reduced and quality improved, and Southwire became the first FPL "Quality Vendor." The companies worked together, and Southwire used statistical process control techniques to become a "Certified Vendor," the first supplier to achieve that status. The partnering did not stop there; Southwire increased its sales to FPL from $400,000 in 1984 to $20.3 million in 1990, while reducing its internal costs because of a lower failure rate. Add in the improved relationship and mutual understanding and the Southwire/FPL partnering has been a true win-win alliance.

Baxter Healthcare Corporation has developed similar partnering arrangements with Monsanto and the West Company (Auld, 1990). Termed a "value managed relationship," Baxter describes its version as "a partnership with a supplier that is dedicated to managing value into both parties' operations on an ongoing basis." Although the company's internal documents supporting the process state the need to "manage our suppliers," the Baxter system demonstrates a willingness to work with its sources to reach mutually beneficial objectives.

Baxter started with West in 1985 to develop special formulations of rubber products, particularly in the parenteral arena. West eventually became the first certified and preferred supplier in the Baxter qualification chain of ten steps. During the certification process, defects per million were reduced from 35,000 to under 200. Field complaints had a ten-fold decline. Rejects on incoming materials went from 19 percent to zero, with returns also going to zero. West was rewarded with a 100 percent increase in volume and also benefited from the declining costs of returns and replacement.

With Monsanto, Baxter followed this concept: "partnerships require that customers and suppliers are cooperative and willing to share information and technology that was once considered proprietary." The results from this alliance of multibillion dollar firms include "mutual, long-term, bottom-line benefits from purchase order consolidation, specific product sourcing, technical support, and invoice accuracy." For example, David Auld, vice-president of Baxter's quality leadership process group, described a mutually beneficial electronic arrangement. "Monsanto used to issue 1,000 purchase orders per month to Baxter. Baxter would issue Monsanto 1,000 invoices in response. This represented a correspondingly large investment in time and dollars for both companies. Primarily because of a quality partnership with Baxter, 1,000 invoices per month were reduced to one summary invoice a week. All of the essential information is now transferred by computer for rapid invoice management for both companies. These results could not have been achieved if business had been conducted solely on a price basis; they were the result of an effective quality partnership."

From Concept to Action

Those organizations with partnering efforts moving in the right direction know where they are going and what it takes to get there. Their objectives are the simple, logical results of a dedicated and mutual effort to gain competitive advantage:

Suppliers Are Invited to Participate in the Planning Process

Where new developments are part of that process, the suppliers have people of equal status sitting next to the customer's researchers and designers. The expectation is that meaningful discussions will result that help the customer get the best innovation in the shortest possible time. In one example from our experience, we were able to place designers and engineers on a customer's panel examining how to cut cycle time for new product introduction. This panel was made up of all of the key suppliers identified in the cycle time "map" that traced the process flow from idea conception to product on the shelf. The first effort by this panel cut the original cycle by 50 percent. They are now working on another 50 percent reduction.

Similar opportunities exist for interactions between the supplier's design team and the buyer's marketing group to improve the presentation of the total offering to the ultimate customer. That means the supplier is invited to make improvement suggestions that will increase the appeal of its customer's products or services. It also means the supplier can be linked to advertising and promotional efforts.

The Entire Network Seeks Customer Satisfaction as Each Interconnection Is Viewed as a Supplier-User System

At every link in the total system, the word *customer* is used as a check to see if the correct needs have been satisfied and a process of continuous improvement has been instituted. That means an information systems group will be asking: who are our customers? What do we supply them? Do they need what we supply? How can we be proactive to help improve what they need to do?

The human resources department will be seeking the core organizational capabilities that need improving, as identified in concert with actual practitioners. Engineering will be working with the rank-and-file assemblers to make sure its designs are user-friendly. Researchers check the feasibility of their concepts with people in the manufacturing process. In all of these interactions, there is understanding of the ultimate consumer's needs and what it takes to "delight" those consumers.

Employees Throughout the Network Understand the Importance of Their Role and Share in the Benefits

As skills are improved to better meet customer requirements and sales increases are documented, workers see an increase in take-home pay. Gainsharing becomes a feature as the link between higher skills and sales translates into a chase for best-in-class performances. Bonuses are not just one-time rewards for short-term effort but become ways to tie reward and recognition to attainment of stretch objectives, on a continuous basis.

Jobs that need to be redesigned are recast by workers, supervisors, and human resources personnel together. Through this alliance, workers become more meaningful, have greater value to the network, and are provided opportunities to exercise their latent capabilities and influence decision making.

The Network Attains Technical Superiority over Its Competition

All of the support functions within the network focus on customer needs and bring the fruits of technology to each customer-supplier intersection. The result is leading-edge status in terms of systems, procedures, error-free communications, methodology, strategy, and implementation.

Depending on whom we interviewed, achieving such lofty objectives is envisioned as a three-to-ten-year quest. From our perspective, there is no timetable. The biggest problem is starting a sincere effort, followed by living the tenets of the process. Our advice is to undertake pilot operations to prove the viability of the tenets and to progress much as a large jigsaw puzzle is built, adding a new piece each day.

We quickly add to that advice that the honest, open, and mutual environment we espouse is the most difficult outcome to achieve. For that reason, we become reinspired by a comment made by John Pughe (Farrell, 1990) of Allied Corporation. He stated: "We want them [our suppliers] to understand our market and where we want to be in that market. We take suppliers right into our forecasting module so they can read what our requirements are: what the first six months are, what's tentative for the next six months, and what our planning is for the next two or three years. We want to rely on them to keep us competitive and put components right into the assembly line to save us the cost of incoming or receiving inspection labor." If Pughe had added "and we want them to prosper in the process," he would have captured the essence of partnering.

At this point, let us see how Alice Harper is accomplishing the move from concept to action as she tries again to move partnering toward the customer.

Alice Goes Proactive

Alice's first reaction to the loss of a major customer was to reward a competitor of that customer. That move would have accomplished little more than to dramatically raise the break-even point on her supply-

demand chart. Instead, after she calmed down, she asked each member of the sales department to submit a list of potential partnering candidates. Her strategy was to select the best of these candidates and to proactively seek a major position. From Alice's perspective, it was now time to seek out customers for partnering, rather than waiting to be asked to participate on the customer's terms.

"We should look for customers who will give us an honest chance at a sole-supplier position," Alice told her Sales Manager, "if we prove our organization has the ability to develop extra values . . . beyond the price negotiations."

"Alice," the Sales Manager replied patiently, "you must be some kind of martyr. The big buyers want price, price, price. That's what you'll find. It's the little companies that will let you make a profit."

Alice sighed. "You may be right, but I'm tired of cutting my own prices to get extra volume. Find me the targets, and together we'll find a customer who wants some help locating extra value."

"I'll play Sancho Panza for awhile," quipped the Sales Manager.

After several months spent sifting through the arguments advanced for each candidate and many preliminary discussions with interested firms, Alice and her direct reports settled on a list of five target accounts. What happened with one of these customers was typical of the approach taken by Alice's organization to form a meaningful alliance with a sincerely interested company.

The initial steps were concentrated on a "vertical slice" of contacts: there was direct interaction between representatives of Alice's unit and the customer, from hourly employees through senior officers. During these interactions, the involved parties at all levels became familiar with both organizations and initiated sincere searches for extra values.

"We want to find the means to improve any facet of our relationship," the Senior Vice-President had told Alice's group. "If that means we challenge a lot of old ideas, let's do it."

Alice had agreed and added to her instructions, "Let's look for any way possible to improve quality, service, delivery, response, cycle time, and cut the costs of doing business together."

The critical aspects of the eventual alliance—later formalized by a five-year contract—were developed at the penultimate meeting of the *negotiating representative of both organizations. Alice and her Sales Manager were supported at that meeting by the Customer Service Manager and the lead hourly associate who had visited the customer's facilities. The customer was represented by the Vice-President of Logistics, the Quality Director, Purchasing Director, and a representative plant manager.*

Toward the end of the meeting, the Logistics Vice-President suggested, "Why don't you summarize your offering, Alice."

"All right," she responded. "In exchange for a position of not less than 75 percent of your volume, we will provide the following: there will be no need for incoming inspection as all product will meet or exceed your quality standards, as verified by statistical data submitted by the crews for each production run."

"Should there be any problems," the Quality Director asked, "what will you do?"

"We will replace the shipment within twenty-four hours and reimburse you for lost manufacturing time," responded Alice.

"That puts the pressure on us to do it right," added the hourly associate. "Our name goes out with these control sheets."

Resuming her presentation, Alice went to the next point. "Deliveries will be made within the specific time frame requested and not later than seventy-two hours after order placement. Inventory will be reduced to one load of safety stock per item."

"We will use the space that formerly housed the inventory for manufacturing purposes," the Logistics Vice-President remarked.

"Next," Alice continued, "we will form a value-enhancement team. Members will come from both companies and be rotated quarterly. The purpose will be to search for savings within our system."

"Tell me where these teams will start," the Purchasing Director asked.

"My suggestion is that we start with your customers and work backward to our operations," Alice responded. "If the teams watch how the end user selects your product and start asking questions right there, they can chase down improvements wherever they make sense. It might be in displaying the product, stocking, handling, warehousing . . . who knows. Our experience has been that whenever a team challenges the way things are done, they usually find a way to do it better."

"Shouldn't they develop a priority list?" asked the Quality Director.

"Absolutely," Alice answered. "These teams typically find lots of opportunities. We should form a steering council to help them decide the priorities, so we know where to put the resources."

Both groups continued to discuss the details of the impending alliance for almost a full day. For each offering, Alice asked and received a commitment for cooperation and shared resources. Better forecasting was offered by the customer, so JIT deliveries could be made. Access to manufacturing data was agreed to as part of the electronic data interchange, when Alice agreed to put her costs into the system and price new items directly by formula. The customer agreed to turn Alice's trucks around faster, when she agreed to inventory slow-turnover items of crucial parts. To help shorten cycle time, the customer granted Alice a position on its market development committee. Numerous small issues were commissioned for resolution by an empowered, joint subcommittee.

"Well, I think that concludes all the big issues," the Logistics Vice-President said. "We'll turn the agreement over to legal. If they have no problem, we can have a signing next week."

Alice and her group thanked the customer and made one final assurance of their desire to make the alliance a success.

"It will succeed," the Purchasing Director responded. "Because we both win in this one."

Action Study: Testing the Idea

To illustrate our point that partnering is a difficult journey that is best moved forward on a pilot basis, we describe a personal experience.

The situation begins in a midwest city where one of our factory managers was requesting capital funds to build a new warehouse. The manager was soliciting approval on the basis of the need to satisfy a large customer that insisted on having product delivered from a convenient warehouse. Our role was to determine if the appropriation should be approved or, more important, if there was a way to satisfy the customer without building a warehouse.

Our initial contact with the customer revealed the source of the warehousing request. The customer was determined that our product would be delivered just-in-time for its manufacturing needs, and made this a requisite for our sustaining and increasing position with the account. One competitor had already agreed to this requirement by securing space in a nearby public warehouse. Our appeal to try JIT deliveries direct from our machines, without the intermediate holding position, was met with adamant refusal.

"If you don't warehouse, you don't get the business," was the curt response.

"All right," was our reply. "Will you try an experiment?"

"What kind of experiment?" was the reluctant response.

"We will secure public warehouse space within a reasonable distance of your facility. We will put into that warehouse sufficient product to meet your needs on *all* items for the next thirty calendar days. In that way, you may visit, touch, or talk to your inventory."

"Don't get funny!" we were reprimanded.

"But for the next ninety days, we will ship your requirements directly from our machines. If, for any reason, we fail to meet your needs in this way, we will immediately pull the product from inventory. In that way, we will still satisfy your JIT requirements."

"What do you expect to prove?" the customer asked.

"That you will never have to go to that warehouse for product. What we put in it at the beginning of the period will be there at the end of the test. Will you try it?"

Somewhat reservedly, the buyer agreed to the test.

"It won't work" was the pronouncement as we booked space and filled it with the appropriate inventory.

For thirty, sixty, ninety days, we managed to ship product just-in-time to meet the customer's manufacturing needs. The buyer remained reluctant to accept the test results. It became apparent to us that the buyer's reluctance was driven by fear of being accused by manufacturing of having a supplier who shut down a process. Here is where we learned of the problem of asking more of suppliers than you do of your own system. The buyer's manufacturing group was unwilling to actively participate in the test to see if the warehousing cost could be eliminated from the system. All manufacturing wanted was perfect product, when needed, in the exact quantity they decided to run at any particular time. While we were willing to do that, we implied that a little cooperation would be advantageous to both parties.

With much perseverance, the test was extended and extended, until the customer removed the requirement for warehousing. Our factory manager recalled the request for a permanent warehouse. The customer responded with a larger volume position, and we all learned a valuable lesson in what it takes to make partnering a reality.

Summary

Historically, customer and supplier exist as two separate and very distinct entities—each shrouded in secrecy and pursuing its own self-interest. Relationships may develop over long time frames, but real interactions are limited in scope and number of participants. Most communication that does occur transpires between the customer's purchasing office and the supplier's sales representatives or customer service department.

Ironically, this traditional business posture limits the ability of both parties to optimize their business results. As each organization acts in its self-interest, nothing occurs to strengthen the total competitive network. In any business, there are networks of suppliers-customers-users that are competing with similar networks. When most communication in these networks revolves around pricing and expediting issues, there is little time left to work on improving quality, inventory, mutual productivity, innovation, and cycle times and to capture all the hidden savings that reside in most of these networks. Organizations need to overcome this shortsighted view and realize the mutual aspects of a business relationship dedicated to continually improving the network. That is the way a competitive advantage is attained.

For those interested in optimizing the use of their valuable resources, we pose three questions:

- Isn't it more logical that business optimization is more likely to occur through open lines of communication and closer working relationships between customer and supplier?
- Isn't it beneficial for the supplier to see how its product or service is used and for the customer to view and understand the supplier's production process?
- Wouldn't it be rewarding to apply the mutual resources and abilities of both organizations to enhance both supplier and customer profitability?

The answer to these questions is "yes." Business optimization is a simple study of logic, complicated by nonenactment. The questions we have posed attack that complication and point out the benefits of business partnering. Open communications and good information exchange on all facets of improvement opportunity are the foundations for business optimization.

Chapter Ten

◆

PARTNERING
IN ACTION

Where can business partnering take an organization? How much progress can be made? Will competitive advantage be sustained? Will the alliances endure? These are questions that can be answered only after partnering is accepted as a concept and the tenets are put into action by a dedicated network that will sustain the effort over the long term. Our own experiences have been very positive. Our portfolio of other organizational successes grows monthly, and we eagerly await the continuing flow of results that will answer our questions. Let us consider where business partnering can proceed.

Results of Successful Implementation

Picture a business network characterized by interchanges of products and services so free of mistakes and defects that rework, returns, and complaints are virtually nonexistent. The occasional, unintentional mishap is quickly corrected and the system improved so it doesn't occur again. Consider that within this environment, the people—from the newest hire to the most senior officer—are trying their best at all times not only to sustain this enviable level of quality but to make improvements wherever possible. Imagine further that this network has attained these levels of performance:

- Safety conditions have been at the zero level of injury and lost time for over two years.

- New products and services are introduced faster than any competitor because cycle time—from idea to commercial success—has been reduced to unprecedented short durations.
- All deliveries of goods and services are made or provided when needed, in the quantities required for optimum lot size production, and with quality that is necessary to keep and delight the customer.
- Modifications to product design, changes to specifications, and new order pricing and scheduling are entered between network systems electronically with unerring accuracy. Forecasts, cost data, terms, and billings are similarly handled in a paperless environment.
- Prices for the products and services necessary to sustain the network have been established contractually, in an atmosphere of trust. Zero inflation has been attained as an objective due to the shared savings regularly generated by the joint value teams working within the network to reduce operating costs.
- Productivity within the system exceeds meaningful benchmarks of performance, set from industry best-accepted practices. Employees generate forty to fifty usable ideas per person per year and have joined together as one team to enhance the viability of the alliances that constitute the network by optimizing the use of all resources.
- All support systems are proactive and customer responsive, which enhances the capabilities of the network through accurate diagnosis and communication of potential improvement techniques.

Finally, consider that common goals guide the workings of the network toward total satisfaction of the ultimate consumer and all intermediary customers, at costs that will ensure the stability and profitability of the constituents. Then imagine how difficult it would be to compete against such an alliance. Imagine the strength of the partners of that alliance to survive and prosper into the future.

We have conjured up an image of the potential outcomes of successful business partnering. As improbable as this picture might appear, a review of the processes that can produce such accomplishment reveals that simple, logical efforts—in terms of doing the right things right, at the right time—are the prime requirements for successful implementation. The totality of the necessary methods and procedures to make the system work may seem overwhelming. The difficulties are not insurmountable; within most business systems, at some moment in time, all of the required elements are present, perhaps only at various points within the network. True benefit arrives when exemplary performances occur consistently across the full spectrum of a business system.

Such performance is possible, but it requires the construction of a mutually acceptable model that will inspire action and the supportive leadership that will make attainment feasible. World-class status can be reached—at a plant, in a department, or across an organization. The journey will have many pitfalls and will present many opportunities to give up the effort. At those crossroads, leaders have to step forward to keep the implementation alive and moving in the correct direction. The reward will be unprecedented levels of personal satisfaction that accrues only from outstanding achievement.

Alice Harper and her associates enjoyed a measure of that satisfaction, as we see in our last visit. We find our heroine savoring the recognition that comes with making our imagined success her reality.

The Fruits of Success for Alice

Alice and her managers were enjoying the flight home on the corporate airplane. The noise of the engines made conversation difficult, but the euphoric passengers did not seem to mind. They had been to the corporate offices to receive the Chairman's Award for best operation in

*the system. The praise heaped on them during the presentation and din-
ner was still fresh in their minds.*

*"They said some great things about us," the Sales Manager grinned
and, with a glass raised toward Alice, added, "Here's to our leader."*

*Alice acknowledged the toast and beamed a grateful smile. "We
make a good team," she enthused. "They said nice things about all of
us. I guess these are the moments that make it all worthwhile."*

*"I'll tell you, Alice," the Production Manager said with a shrug.
"When we lost the Excellent business to Gilroy, I thought we were dead.
Who would have believed we could replace that kind of volume two
fold?"*

*"I knew we could do it," the Sales Manager interjected. "It was
just a matter of time!"*

*"What surprised me was the margins on the new business," the
Accounting Manager mused. "In the past, if we replaced that much
volume, we'd go into the tank for a year . . . take us twelve to eighteen
months to get the margins back."*

*"We got the margins," the Sales Manager said, "by sticking to our
game plan and selling value . . . showing our customers how to save
money, on a permanent basis. I'll bet everything I own that Gilroy has
been raising prices on Excellent every chance they get, and doing it
without the customer knowing it's happening. Only way they could
survive."*

*"Forget about Gilroy, and Excellent. You got the business, and the
margins, because you started selling service," the Customer Service Manager disagreed. "I talk to those customers. Some of them still can't believe we do what we do. We made it easy for them to do business with
us by keeping all of our promises. Now they want our products, our
attention, our service, our ideas . . . and they don't mind if we make
a profit doing it."*

*"A reasonable profit," Alice reminded. She looked thoughtfully out
the window. "Yes, it took over a year to recover, and a lot of work, but
the results were worth it." She returned her attention to her managers.
"I'll never forget my feelings when we lost Excellent, after all the things
we did for them. I wanted to hurt them, help their competition. But
then I remembered what they told me. We had been paid for the busi-*

ness they gave us. We just had to find someone who would pay for the values I knew we could deliver . . . and we did. I'm grateful to all of you for keeping me on the right track and not letting me give away the store in a fit of anger."

"You were easy to calm down," the Sales Manager complimented. "We all knew it wouldn't do any good to try and hurt Excellent."

"It was just the way they kept assuring us they wanted new ideas, new techniques," Alice sighed.

"That's water over the dam," the Sales Manager said. "We found the right customers."

The Production Manager nodded agreement. "And we built a strong network. We've made costs go away for our customers by using our brains, not a sharp pencil."

The Accounting Manager nodded agreement. "We're saving our customers a lot of money . . . and they're helping us, too. Those low costs and higher efficiencies the chairman cited were helped by our partners."

"Yes, they were," Alice agreed, "but before we get too complacent about our success, let's remember we have a tough act to sustain. A whole year without a single return or late delivery is fantastic, but now our partners expect repeat performances."

"We also have to remember there's somebody out there chasing us," the Sales Manager added. "We took business away from some people who will be trying hard to get it back."

Alice raised her glass toward the group. "Well," she said, "if we want to be the first repeat winner of the Chairman's Award, we have to keep improving our network. Here's to the real meaning of partnering— inside and outside—and the people who made it happen."

Closing in on Reality

As we conducted our research on organizations that were pursuing business partnering, we were encouraged by those we saw moving toward a world-class model. We were also impressed by their willingness to share the secrets of their success. Florida Power and Light, 3M, Motorola, Xerox, and Milliken are beacons that can lead the way to outstanding achievement. These organizations have unselfishly communicated the concepts and disciplines that led to their implementation of improvements that proved elusive to similar firms. Other firms like IBM-Rochester, Emerson Electric, AT&T, Baxter, Corning, Du Pont, Tenneco, Texas Instruments, and Westinghouse have also shared their experiences, good and bad, so a model of success could be generated for others to follow.

The Japanese continue to set new levels of accomplishment that raise the benchmarks for those firms that want to be the best-of-the-best. Many more organizations we studied (and certainly others we were not able to contact) have achieved success with their versions of partnering. Networks are forming as these stories are circulated and discussed. Professional organizations such as the American Society for Quality Control (ASQC), the Quality and Productivity Management Association (QPMA), the American Productivity and Quality Center (APQC), the Association for Quality and Participation (AQP), and many other dedicated societies are striving to increase the networking by providing forums for presentations of the successes. Those companies that want to make progress now have many avenues from which to choose to develop the necessary guidelines.

We conclude that within the business community of North America there is sufficient knowledge, dedication, and understanding of how to use continuous improvement to create stronger, more competitive, and more satisfying alliances that such improvement can become reality—for those willing to make the concerted effort. The end results will be greater customer satisfaction, increased job security on national scales, more effective utilization of all resources, and substantially greater job satisfaction. Business partnering is one key to establishing and nurturing the networks that will create those results. There are many more. The basic requirement is the realization of the strength of individual effort combined in teams working together for mutual benefit. It requires people willing to give as much as they take from the alliance. It requires trust and faith in those people's abilities. In that sense, we offer business partnering as a success strategy for the 1990s.

References

"AMEX Life Takes the Quality Road to a New Corporate Vision." *Commitment Plus Newsletter*, Quality & Productivity Management Association, March 1991, pp. 1–4.

Anderluh, J. R. "From Vision to Decision and Back Again." Paper presented at Quality & Productivity Management Association Fall Conference, St. Louis, Mo., September 1990.

Auld, D. "Baxter Healthcare Corporation Applies Innovative Approach to Customer/Supplier Partnerships." Paper presented at the Quality in Services Conference, Norwalk, Conn., July 1990.

Camp, W. *Benchmarking: The Search for Industry Best Practices That Lead to Superior Performance.* Milwaukee, Wis.: ASQC Quality Press, 1979.

Cayer, S. "Why Reinvent the Wheel?—Interview with Kenneth Stork, Motorola." *Purchasing Magazine*, Jan. 17, 1991, pp. 89–91.

Colgate-Palmolive Supplier Conference: "Realizing Our Potential Together." New York, January 1991.

Conway, J. "Partnerships: A Bottom-Line Approach to Business." *CPI Purchasing*, Mar. 1991, pp. 34–39.

Crosby, P. B. *Quality Is Free.* New York: McGraw-Hill, 1979.

Deming, W. E. *Out of the Crisis.* Cambridge, Mass.: MIT Press, 1982.

Ephlin, D. "How to Get Union Leaders and Members Involved in TQM." Paper presented at Quality & Productivity Management Association Fall Conference, St. Louis, Mo., September 1990.

Farrell, P. V. "Purchasing into the 90's . . . and Beyond." *Purchasing World Magazine,* Jan. 1990, pp. 27–29.

Feigenbaum, A. *Total Quality Control.* New York: McGraw-Hill, 1989.

Feigenbaum, A. "Quality: The Pioneers Survey the Landscape." *Industry Week,* Oct. 21, 1991, p. 69.

Florida Power and Light. "World-Class Excellence." With American Productivity & Quality Center (Houston, Tex.), October 1990.

General Electric. "GE-TAPP, Global Excellence–Through Applied Productivity Partnering." Conference sponsored by GE as part of quality certification program, Cleveland, Ohio, March 1991.

Ginnodo, W., executive director of QPMA. Remarks on presenting USAA with the Quality & Productivity Management Association (QPMA) 1991 Leadership Award.

Goldratt, E. M. *The Goal.* Croton-on-Hudson, N.Y.: North River Press, 1984.

Goldratt, E. M., and Fox, R. E. *The Race.* Croton-on-Hudson, N.Y.: North River Press, 1986.

Gordon, N. "Supplier Quality Partnership Program." Paper presented at ASQC Quality Congress Transactions, San Francisco, 1990.

Gross, I. "Partnering: Games Businesses Play." *Marketplace: The ISBM Review,* Pennsylvania State University, Spring 1989, pp. 1–5.

Hardie, N. "Leadership Through Quality." Paper presented at Quality & Productivity Management Association Fall Conference, St. Louis, Mo., September 1990.

Hooker, S. P. "Performance Development." Paper presented at Quality & Productivity Management Association Spring Conference, Chicago, April 1991.

Imai, M. *Kaizen: The Key to Japan's Competitive Success.* New York: Random House, 1986.

Juran, J. "Strategies for World-Class Quality." *Quality Progress,* Mar. 1991, pp. 81–85.

Kearney, A. T., Inc. *Seeking and Destroying the Wealth Dissipators.* Chicago: A. T. Kearney, Inc., 1985.

Klassen, J. "Service Excellence at Royal Bank." *Commitment Plus Newsletter,* Quality & Productivity Management Association, Oct. 1988, p. 3.

McAdory, W. C. "Lessons Learned About Total Quality." *Tapping the Network Journal,* Quality & Productivity Management Association, Summer 1991, pp. 2–4.

Ohno, T. *Kanban: Just-In-Time at Toyota.* Cambridge, Mass.: Productivity Press, 1986.

Peters, T. *Thriving on Chaos.* New York: Knopf, 1987.

Peters, T. J., and Waterman, R. H. *In Search of Excellence.* New York: HarperCollins, 1982.

"Preston Profits by Dancing with the Bear." *Commercial Carrier Journal,* Feb. 1990, pp. 74–80.

Pughe, J. Moderator at roundtable sponsored by *Purchasing World Magazine,* 1990.

Shingo, S. *A Revolution in Manufacturing: The SMED System.* Cambridge, Mass.: Productivity Press, 1985.

"Statistical Comparisons." *International Productivity Journal,* Fall 1991, p. 78.

Teal, T. "Service Comes First: An Interview with USAA's Robert F. McDermott." *Harvard Business Review,* Sept.–Oct. 1991, pp. 116–127.

Wratten, R. W. "Accountability, Teams and Rewards: Three Keys to Improvement." Paper presented at Quality & Productivity Management Association Fall Conference, St. Louis, Mo., September 1990.

Index

This page constitutes a continuation of the copyright page.

Chapter One action study: Harry Shaw's name used by permission.

Chapter Two action study: Used by permission of AMEX Life Assurance Company.

Chapter Three action study: Used by permission of USAA.

Chapter Four action study: Used by permission of Leaf, Inc.

Chapter Five action study: Used by permission of Toyota.

Chapter Six action study: Used by permission of Levi Strauss.

Chapter Seven action study and Figure 7.1: Used by permission of Milliken & Co.

Chapter Eight action study: From the American Society for Quality Control, Inc., 1990. Reprinted by permission.

P. 87: Figure 4.1. Used by permission of The Institute.

P. 205: Figure 9.1. Used by permission of Walker Manufacturing.